For the Record & Off the record

Leadership Lessons from the Music World

Melbourne to Dubai

Revised edition

Copyright © 2024 by Richard Rashid Hussein

All rights reserved.

No part of this book may be reproduced in any form without written permission from the author, except for brief quotations in a review or scholarly work.

Bismillah-ir-Rahman-ir-Rahim
in the name of God, the merciful and compassionate.

This book is dedicated to
Sarah Hussein

Preface

Within these pages, delve into my world, a collection of real-life short stories and experiences, each metamorphosed into a melodic journey. Envision this book as an old vinyl or CD record, adorned with a sticker proudly declaring, "Featuring 40 Hits."

The ensuing chapters unravel my personal history, intricately woven into the dynamic realm of the music business and life. Each story stands as a testament to triumphs and trials, providing not only a glimpse into my life but also a window into the inner workings of the music industry. These tales come to life with a soundtrack of thoughtfully curated music titles, akin to the tracks on a cherished album. It's essential to note that while these songs align with the themes of each chapter, they don't necessarily represent my personal favourites.

This concise book is a heartfelt gift to my daughter, Sarah M. Hussein, crafted to impart a profound understanding of my journey through the past. Beyond our family narrative, my aspiration is for these tales to resonate with others, inspiring them to persist in their pursuits, even when the world seems indifferent.

In sharing these stories, it's not a tell-all-the-music industry insider book, as that might be very interesting and perhaps for another time. My intention is not to boast but to offer readers the potential for inspiration. I aim to convey the message that the path to achieving one's goals is a non-linear journey, accessible to anyone with determination. Through these narratives, I aspire to instil positive change and success, making a meaningful contribution to the realms of business and elite mental coaching.

Within this musical journey, I'll harness the power of my world of music metaphors and the transformative L.I.O.N model that I have created to hopefully add value to the lives of those seeking inspiration and transformation, not only in the music business but in life itself.

Richard Rashid Hussein.

Artist: Richard Rashid Hussein.

Album title: For the Record & Off the record. Leadership Lessons from the Music World

Feat 40 hit lessons from Melbourne to Dubai

The below is my L.I.O.N model that has been inspired out my experiences in life and my studies in the N.L.P world, I want to help people **L**ead, **I**nspire, **O**wn the outcomes and **N**urture for positive change,

- Leading high performance and powerful mindset shifts
- Inspiring- reframe and redirection of the neural pathways
- Outcomes driven for optimum transformation
- Nurturing the ongoing unconscious shifts and positive changes

Credits: Author & composer-Richard Rashid Hussein (mind fitness coach, hypnotist, entertainment and business entrepreneur) M.B.M and certified NLP practitioner.

Recorded in Lionheart studios Dubai, mixed and mastered by Richard Rashid Hussein Melbourne, Australia.

Book artwork by Saim Ahmed, Book concept ideas from Sarah Hussein and Richard Rashid Hussein.

Copyright Richard Rashid Hussein 2024

Start date Dubai, June 2021 Dubai,

Completed June 2024 Melbourne.

Introduction

- My Journey and reflection INTRO- Running (song inspires)
- My journey till date
- Melodies and swag growing up around music
- Start me up
- Leaving EMI Music - The Corporate Life
- "Seeds of Manifestation: A Journey from Career Planning to Mentoring Success in Music and Beyond"
- The now and the Future.

THE TRACKLIST CHAPTERS

1. Connected.
2. Ice Ice Baby (Alright Stop. Collaborate and Listen.)
3. More Than A Feeling.
4. Don't Stop Believing.
5. Sweet Child O Mine.
6. Come Together (Right now.. over me.)
7. What a Fool Believes, Growth, Relationships.
8. When The Going Gets Tough, The Tough Gets Going.
9. Walk Of Life.
10. I Did It My Way.
11. Let It Be (there will be an answer.)
12. The Show Must Go On.
13. Every Little Thing Is Gonna Be Alright.
14. Don't Leave Me This Way.
15. Everyone's A Winner.
16. Firework.
17. All I Need Is A Miracle.
18. Superfreak.
19. Causing A Commotion.
20. Heartbreaker.
21. Upside Down.
22. I Gotta Feeling.
23. I'll Be There.: Leadership and Resolve.
24. Ain't No Mountain High Enough: Customer Obsession.
25. Let's Dance: Finding Harmony in Business.
26. New Rules: Bridging Business Cultures.
27. Price Tag: Upholding Integrity.

28. Crazy: Think outside the box, you just never know.
29. Invisible Touch: Lessons from a misjudged Album.
30. Hotel California: Lessons from Rockstar Antics.
31. With a Little Help from My Friends: Navigating Retail Challenges.
32. Everybody Hurts: Navigating Product Placement Pitfalls.
33. It's Not Over Yet : Adapting to Shifting Perception.
34. Walk Like an Egyptian : Navigating Egypt's Business Culture.
35. Another One Bites the Dust: Navigating the Ethical Borders.
36. Respect.
37. Gold.
38. Faith.
39. Never Gonna Give You Up.
40. The Time Of My Life.
41. Encore chapter. "Unbelievable."
42. Album credits and Thank you
43. Biography for Richard Rashid Hussein

QR Code- For the record & Off the record chapter soundtrack.

These tracks are not necessarily personal favourites however they are songs that resonate with each chapter describing each story. For copyright reasons I have not added the Artists names in each chapter.

QR Code- Richard Rashid Hussein 20 years of Arabic songs that he has worked on including signed, licenced, exported, A & R or produced. This is not a complete list as there are many songs that are not found on the platform. I hope you enjoy them.

To contact Richard Rashid Hussein,
Email @ RICHARDHUSSEIN1@GMAIL.COM

My journey and reflection
INTRO- Running (song inspires)

"In my perspective, the transformative influence of music extends far beyond entertainment; it has the profound ability to shape our emotions, thoughts, and even our personalities. As an elite mental performance coach, music business entrepreneur, and former DJ, I've had the privilege of witnessing the remarkable power of music to alter moods and create shared experiences among diverse audiences. This universal language, however, transcends personal expression and emotion; it also plays a pivotal role in the world of business.

My journey in the music business, intricately woven with my DJ skills, has provided me with a unique vantage point. From crafting playlists that elevate a crowd's experience in a venue to nurturing artists from bedroom studios to global streaming platforms and leveraging the strategic use of music in marketing campaigns, my experiences have unveiled the symbiotic relationship between music and business success. This book is a culmination of my life's experiences and industry insights, a guide that seeks to bridge the gap between strategic applications in the world of music business and their relevance in addressing everyday life challenges.

Building upon this foundation, my journey took an unexpected yet immensely rewarding turn. Today, I am a certified mental fitness coach with a diverse range of clients. I have seamlessly integrated the profound experiences from the world of music and life into a structured program—a program that follows three simple yet powerful steps: Discovery, Action, and Nurturing. I call this program the L.I.O.N Model, where each step embodies the essence of Leading, Inspiring, Owning, and Nurturing.

The LION Model, developed through my experiences as a certified mental fitness coach, serves as a testament to the universal applicability of music's transformative power. Through this model, I guide individuals through three fundamental steps. First, the Discovery phase encourages self-exploration, unlocking hidden potentials and passions. Next, the Action phase prompts decisive steps toward personal and professional goals, mirroring the rhythm and momentum found in a well-curated playlist. Finally, the Nurturing phase fosters a continuous cycle of growth and well-being, akin to the harmonious progression of a musical composition.

As we delve into the following chapters, I'll unravel the threads that connect my diverse roles in the music industry, DJaying, and mental fitness coaching. Together, we'll explore how the rhythms of music and how some of the principles of the L.I.O.N Model intertwine to offer practical insights for navigating the complex symphony of life's challenges. Whether you're in pursuit of artistic expression, business success, or personal growth, the harmony of music, entrepreneurship, and mental fitness holds valuable lessons for all.

Join me on this journey as we navigate the intersections of passion, business, and personal development, guided by the transformative beats that echo through every facet of life. As we explore the harmonies that resonate beyond the confines of entertainment, I will share practical knowledge gained from the intersection of my music business endeavours and DJ expertise, offering a unique perspective on how these realms can harmonize to amplify success and fulfillment in both your professional and personal endeavours."

My journey till date. (The boy from Newport, Melbourne, Australia)

    Let me first start by sharing a bit about me and my name and its origins before my journey. My family is from Lebanon and our ancestors are from Jbeil (Byblos) originally, who later moved to the north of Lebanon and then my parents migrated to Australia in the late 1960's. I was born in Carlton and raised in Newport Melbourne, Australia, as Rashid Hussein (Rash), I faced an identity challenge with such an exotic name. As a kid, my teachers often struggled to pronounce "Rashid," resorting to calling me Richard instead. This led to me officially changing my name to Richard Hussein in my teens.

    Growing up, I was unconsciously not proud of my original name, however as I got older, I began to appreciate the beauty of my Arabic name. "Rashid" means "rightly guided, having the true faith," and I was named after my grandfather, which adds a layer of personal significance. My name Richard often puzzled people as they tried to guess my religious background. I would frequently receive puzzled looks when people saw my surname, unsure if I was Muslim or Christian. I guess this gave me uniqueness, and I'm proud to have both names. Additionally, I am proud of my heritage, embracing both my Arabic roots and the Australian culture I was raised in.

    As a kid finding his identity in a very rough and tough suburb of Melbourne named Newport, I grew up in an era where there were a lot of gangs, violence, graffiti and you learnt to be very street smart in my suburb. This was the 80s and society in ways was reflecting in its own ways what was happening in the

United States with the time in the era of movies like "colors", "new jack city" etc and in my view my suburb was very renowned for this in comparison to today in which it has become an up and coming affluent suburb. Those who grew up in that era and were from Melbourne may remember the name the Newport Boys and they may know how uber cool yet dangerous this suburb really was. Although it was dangerous we learnt a lot of positives out of it including loyalty, leadership and learning to be strong. My childhood was a little different than other Lebanese kids in my area, we had a small family which is unusual for big Lebanese families, and I dealt with having parents' divorce when I was young which at that time was extremely different for my community. My family was very encultured and had a good mix of Australian and Middle East culture. We did what most kids did in that era, play at the park with around 20-30 other kids on weekends that included cricket or footy depending on the season and we grew our community with loyalty. I am so proud of my community and to date I see people who I have known for many decades that are still dear to me. I grew up in an era where we were still in a simple time with less gadgets and more outdoor activities. How lucky was I.

Melodies and swag, growing up around music

I was immersed in a rich tapestry of music that laid the foundation for a lifelong love affair with the art. My father, known in the community as Abu Rashid, was an aspiring musician, who filled our home with the soulful sounds of Arabic melodies. I have vivid memories of evenings when he would record his own songs in the Lebanese traditional Mawal style, a popular Arabic genre characterized by slow beats and sentimental lyrics, onto his reel to reel machine. He would also play music by iconic artists like Oum Kalthoum and Farid al-Attrache in his car, offering an intimate glimpse into his passion and dreams of becoming a performing artist. Although he eventually shifted his focus to support our family, the echoes of his musical aspirations lingered.

My uncle Badir, in his early 20s, who lived with us and became like a second father to me, was a single young man deeply engrossed in his exploration of life. Unknowingly, he introduced me to music as well. He owned a beautiful sports car of the time, a Ford XY, and I fondly recall how he would take my sister and me for drives, exposing us to the trends of the late '70s and early '80s. We listened to iconic soundtracks like "Grease" and "Saturday Night Fever," especially the track "Stayin' Alive," as well as his favourite, "Heart of Glass" by Blondie. Even to this day, these songs remain some of my all-time favourites.

My mother, too, played her part in this symphony of influences. Her weekends were accompanied by the tunes of Arabic songs, a soundtrack to her culinary creations and household chores. These early exposures to the power of music became the bedrock of my affection for the art. It was not merely a soundtrack to our lives; it was an integral part of our identity.

As a child of the '80s, my immersion into the world of music deepened through the influences of an older sister Nada and her best friend, Rita, who I consider my other sister, along with their friends. Our house became a hub for musical discovery, a haven where boys and girls gathered to revel in the sounds of the era. I fondly recall my first album purchase at the age of seven, DEVO's 'Freedom of Choice,' complete with the iconic 'Whip It' hat that I proudly wore in emulation. I used to dance in the backyard, mimicking the track, and sometimes my mother would just look at me and laugh, much to my embarrassment. One of my pleasurable yet traumatic memories was when I used to listen to songs by putting my ear too close to the tape recorder speaker and playing it at maximum volume. One time, while listening to another favourite of the era, "Can You Feel It" by the Jacksons, I think I almost blew out my eardrum. I remember a persistent hum in my ear, which led me to visit the doctor and learn never to put my ear so close again.

As the mid-'80s unfolded, my musical tastes underwent a transformation influenced by the iconic figures of Michael Jackson, Prince, and Madonna. Their magnetic presence in the music scene left an indelible mark on my growing appreciation for the art. Breakdancing, hip-hop, R&B, and rap continued to pulse through my adolescence. Inspired by movies like 'Breakdance' and 'Beat Street,' I found myself captivated by the dance movements, graffiti art, and the infectious energy of the breakdance scene. Hip hop, with its underground allure, became a source of fascination and rebellion."

My mentor, Khol Houli, is perhaps my earliest childhood memory. He was, and still is, like an older brother to me. His family lived with us in the same house while I was still in diapers, and he has had the most profound influence on my life. He was the first to encourage me to venture out of the house and play in the local park when I was 9 years old. He helped set the foundations for me to be compassionate, strong and acquire leadership skills. When I think if he hadn't been in my life, I think I would be a wreck, I think he would say I'm still a wreck (haha), The other key friend who also helped in shaping me whilst growing up was Ziad, again older than me he always kept me on track and was probably smoother than Khol in advice. Khol was brutally honest when I needed it and Ziad a little smoother, although occasionally I would get the wrath from both in order to fix myself. I was extremely lucky to have a few very close friends that pushed each other to become the best versions of themselves.

The thrill of receiving cassette albums from Khol, featuring iconic artists like RUN DMC and Eric B & Rakim, and the subsequent listening sessions with friends, marked a pivotal moment in my musical journey. We couldn't help but wonder, "How is this not popular in Australia?" as we absorbed the unfiltered voices of African American culture, resonating with its messages of identity, struggle, and resilience.

As a pre-teen navigating the challenges of being part of a minority with immigrant parents, the melodies, art, and swagger of artists like RUN DMC, Rakim, and Public Enemy spoke to me on a profound level. The gold chains, the attitude, and the messages they conveyed became more than just music—they were a reflection of my own experiences and struggles.

As I got older into my mid to late teens, I expanded my group of friends and I had two other very close friends that were my age, Khol and Ziad were older than me and were like older brothers and mentors, however my two of my few buddies were Saad and Haythem. I got to hang out with Saad since I was in grade 4 around 10 years of age as we were in the same class and for a very long time, we were inseparable. Haysam was like a relative. Our families were from a similar part in Lebanon and my father and Uncle were close in friendship with his parents. We met when I was around 12 or 13, my dad would take me to their shop they owned in Richmond and once he moved to my area we spent many fun times together. These two guys among others were my age and part of going out and having fun crew, they also were into music however not as much as me, I would hang out with either of them daily and they were at the start of my professional music DJ career and would support me in all my DJ gigs at times they would be there to 5 am in the morning 'till I finished and helping carry my music crates. I am very blessed to have them still feature big time in my life and to be able to call them brothers.

In retrospect, these early encounters with music weren't just a soundtrack to my youth; they were the building blocks of a lifelong journey that would intertwine with my career in the music business and as a DJ. This book is a reflection on those formative years, exploring how experiences of my past continue to resonate in my present and influence my understanding of the in both business and everyday life."

Start me up.

"Armed with my own confidence and swag, I embarked on a journey that took me from a small-time graffiti artist to a dancer with an R&B crew in 1988, performing at various shows and festivals across Melbourne, in those days I was a massive Bobby Brown fan and one of closest childhood friends at that time Helen would tell everyone that I was Melbourne's Bobby Brown, It's so funny when I think about it today, I had the same hairstyle and moves I was teaching the local community dance moves and I was so passionate of the art of dancing. A year later, my fascination with DJaying took centre stage, inspired by the talents of prominent Melbourne DJs, friends of my sister. They supplied me with edited tapes for my dance crew shows, sparking my interest in the art of DJaying.

I vividly remember the day I decided to become a DJ. With excitement coursing through my veins, I purchased my first three 12-inch vinyls from Brash's music retail store in the city—Bell Biv Devoe's 'Poison,' GUY's 'I Wanna Get with U,' and Bobby Brown's 'Every Little Step.' This marked the beginning of a journey that saw me transition from making mixtapes in my bedroom to rocking dance floors at prominent nightclubs and community radio stations. Despite starting with just a dozen records and a couple of hit mixtapes, I hustled my way into the local scene, eventually becoming a well-known name.

The early days of DJaying were a real hustle. Initially, while performing at local parties, and later in nightclubs even though I was underage, I lied about my age to be able to perform in nightclubs. I used to mimic live DJaying with borrowed tapes, acting out the transitions and beats until I could afford to build my record collection. Little did they know I would DJ for free; I was just so passionate about being in front of an audience and gaining experience. This success eventually introduced me to initially radio presenting on various community stations for a short stint and to the world of record labels for almost 30 years.

I remember in the early '90s working in a seedy venue in a prominent suburb of St Kilda, DJaying to three people. This led, in a couple of months, to a packed house with long queues and I soon was scouted to work at a venue called the Grainstore in the city. My friend Dale, with whom I DJayed at the St Kilda venue, got a business card from a record company executive at Warners. This is where we discovered the world of obtaining promotional records to play in venues. We would hustle weekly, visiting record companies when not invited, and claim to be in the area. We asked for the promotional marketing managers with whom we eventually built a relationship to get the latest vinyl records. Looking back, we were so audacious for free records. I remember once walking into Polygram records and meeting a gentleman named John Scott, who later became a friend of mine in Dubai. He unknowingly inspired me for future work in the labels. In those days, the labels were predominantly full of white Australian guys, and although he is Australian, his olive complexion inspired me to say why not me and to believe that perhaps I could do that job in the future, which indeed happened.

DJaying wasn't just a profession; it taught me invaluable lessons in selflessness, understanding people's behaviours on an intricate level, and the importance of studying micro-emotions to keep my dance floor alive. Today, the metaphor of the DJ profession permeates many aspects of my life.

In the mid-'90s, my dear friend Ziad and my sister Nada encouraged me to return to school, leading me to enrol in a music industry course at N.M.I.T. Melbourne. There, I met a long-term friend, Samantha Cameron. This decision became a turning point in my life. In 1996, Samantha and I secured internships at BMG Records. We were immersed in the daily workings of the industry—packaging posters, cutting press clippings, and sending vinyls to DJs. Reflecting on those days, I realized the importance of education in the business world.

Ziad was an important person in my life. A couple of years older and well-educated, he would have deep conversations with me, and to this day, he is an inspiring brother who brings positive change into my life. Samantha and I, aspiring to become movers and shakers in the music business, studied together and constantly listened to music and attended industry events to get a glimpse of the business. Samantha also assisted me in managing small Australian pop bands in the 90's to fast track our on ground business education.

Armed with academic qualifications and DJ experience, my undergraduate degree, marked by outstanding academic results and receiving from the University the Golden Key award for top 15% results, was testament to the guidance of great mentors. They played pivotal roles in shaping my academic journey, laying the foundation for what would become a fulfilling career in the music business.

I was eager to make my mark in the Australian music industry. In the mid-'90s, I was determined to meet Australia's music business icon, Mr. Michael Gudinski (R.I.P). I finally got that opportunity one day at the Crown Casino in Melbourne. There I was, a young guy, who stopped him while he was busy walking and said, "I would like to talk to you." He stopped, and I nervously said that I wanted to work in the music business, jumbling my words and probably not making much sense. He was kind and listened to me, though I'm pretty sure he wouldn't have remembered the encounter, as there were likely many people like me seeking an opportunity. Before I knew it, he kindly said he needed to go and left respectfully.

Fast forward almost 20 years later, I made contact with Gudinski through a friend and Australian music industry legend Michael Chugg who I met in Dubai in 2008. Chuggy as he is known in the industry was Gudinski's business partner and I was telling him about my passion to return home to Melbourne and work in the industry again and with Gudinski and Chuggy arranged a meeting with Gudinski in Melbourne when I would return from Dubai. We scheduled a few meetings and by this time Gudinski was aware of my international success but unfortunately meetings were rescheduled, we never met again as he passed away in 2021.

My relentless pursuit of success led me to my first real employment opportunity in the music industry. In 1999, during the peak of the boy band frenzy with groups like Backstreet Boys and NSYNC, I secured an initial position as a receptionist with Zomba-Jive records, I didn't care about the position, I was finally in the business and working with some of the best in the Industry. My determination was evident as I persistently called the company three times a week for three months, relentlessly expressing my eagerness for a chance until they finally offered me an opportunity.

Working with Zomba-Jive Records was a valuable experience. Immersed in the boy band and pop phenomenon of the late 90's, I learned extensively and collaborated with a wonderful team. Those who know me very well might well perhaps know why I love some of the music from the Backstreet Boys or Britney and this is because we had their music played daily on repeat in the office and for me it was a golden era. The experience of working on major releases like NSYNC's Bye Bye Bye, Backstreet Boys "Shape of my heart" and Britney Toxic were some huge highlights for me in understanding the music machine and in that time and era we as a label were killing it and the industry knew it. My journey took an unexpected turn during my first performance review a year into the job, where the Managing Director, Paul who I owe a lot to for mentoring me in the early days of the Australian Music Industry. Paul asked me in this meeting about my future aspirations. With unwavering confidence, I stated that I aspired to have his job. Although he smirked at my boldness, little did I know that he was strategically grooming me, and I learned so much about the business with him placing me in all departments of the label. Initially, I thought he was punishing me until I realized his wisdom in getting me familiar with different departments in the business. I found myself in various positions within the company—reception, administration, sales—and was instructed to observe without talking during meetings. In hindsight, I realize the comprehensive understanding of the entire business that was imparted, for which I am grateful. On the A&R side, the emphasis was placed on what I feel and steering away from imitation artists whenever possible, always seeking uniqueness in sound with a compelling backstory. I continued this until the merger with BMG in 2002, which resulted in my retrenchment. I felt lost.

      In the pursuit of clarity, I decided to pursue a master's in business. During my studies, I crossed paths with mentors, Dr. Anthony Lowe and Dr. Stephen Downes, who played pivotal roles in shaping my understanding of the business world. Meanwhile, I landed a consulting job with EMI Music Australia, focusing on Arabic and world music content. I had some great success in this role, and it attracted the attention of the Middle East office team when I had a few top 10 charting albums on the local world music charts. I created my own local compilations and released some big Arabic artists for the local market and my big hit was an Album titled Arabia 2moro in which I did a strategic alliance with local Arabic radio station in Sydney, this was the start of my link to the Arabic music world, prior to that I hardly listened to Arabic music. The opportunity arose after establishing a connection with the EMI team during my visit to Lebanon on honeymoon in 2001. This is where I met my future boss Pascal Galliot, who was heading the EMI Lebanon office, and they happened to be the licensee for Zomba/Jive Records at the time. What is funny is how this and things transpired for future work with EMI. Prior I had just come back from Holland where I had visited the Jive records office and where I met a legend of the music business named Martin Dodd at Jive Records and he was behind projects such as Backstreet Boys, Britney, Star Academy etc. I told Martin I was flying to Lebanon, and he said you should bring Star Academy to the Middle East. While in Lebanon, I visited our local office licensee, and Pascal invited me to listen to some of the local signings and I shared the Star Academy idea which eventuated to a big local hit less than a year later. I was so impressed with the local music Pascal was letting me listen to and said this should be released in Australia. Soon after, and after I left Jive records, I found myself working with the same team and releasing the content.

The year 2003 presented significant challenges as I lost both of my parents within 3 months. In the face of adversity, I deferred my studies and continued working on a part-time basis, grappling with the profound changes in my life. Moving forward, I built on my experiences, leading to a major leap in 2006 when I joined EMI Music MENA in Dubai."

I want to express my deep appreciation for the leadership of the country the U.A.E and its leadership that fosters opportunity for success and I acknowledge that it is not without its criticism. In 2006, my life underwent significant changes, marked by the birth of my daughter, Sarah—a moment that remains the greatest gift of my life. Simultaneously, I embarked on a new chapter by relocating to Dubai in Dec 2005 to join EMI Records while also completing my master's thesis.

One thing I would like to mention for the reader is that Dubai and the U.A.E. are very special places. The leadership of H.H. Sheikh Mohammed Bin Rashid and H.H. Sheikh Mohammed

Bin Zayed has created an environment that is unique to the world. The cities are not without differing views and criticism like anything that becomes successful, however for me, they inspire the belief that anyone can achieve something remarkable in that country. I owe so much gratitude to this country, which graciously granted me a Golden visa as it has been my home for almost two decades.

The decision to move to Dubai materialized in August 2005 when the opportunity with EMI Records presented itself. Seeking guidance, I turned to mentors from my past. Their encouragement, along with the promise of references and guidance on enhancing my CV, fuelled my confidence to seize the opportunity. With this newfound self-assurance and a wealth of life experiences, I embraced the challenge and contributed to EMI Records until 2012.

This era holds a special place in my philosophy, primarily due to the profound impact of becoming a father. Sarah's arrival shifted my perspective, reminding me of the importance of life beyond the challenges of work. No matter how demanding my professional responsibilities were, coming home to Sarah grounded me and highlighted the deeper, more significant aspects of life.

My tenure at EMI Music Arabia was an incredible experience, shaped by a fantastic team and colleagues. The collaborative spirit within the organization laid the foundation for lasting relationships that endure to this day. I was so hungry for success and to prove myself in the region and to others in the industry in Australia that I absolutely worked my butt off, I know

now that's probably not the right motivation today however it was mine at that time. When I started at EMI Music Arabia our main competition was Rotana music who had much more money to spend however, we took them on in strategy and in many instances, we beat them. I did the late hours, ate up all the new experiences and networks and frankly at that time I believed I could be the best which gave me huge confidence.

To this day, the memories of this period resonate as a testament to the delicate balance between professional success and the meaningful priorities that family brings into focus."

"Turning art into a big business is a multifaceted journey, and I consider myself fortunate to work on amazing music and that I have learned from some of the best mentors in the industry. Locally, I owe a great deal to my MDs Pascall Galliot & Adrian Cheesley, as well as the finance team, especially TD for his ever-continuing words of wisdom. Their guidance and the opportunity to work my dream job are invaluable. "I consider myself truly blessed to have been part of the golden era of Arabic music. During that period, I managed a catalogue that featured the legends of Arabic music, such as Oum Kalthoum, Farid Al Attrache, Abdel Halem Hafez, Fairuz, Wassouf, Kadim Al Sahir and Warda – providing me with both an education and an introduction to the greatest music of that region. Simultaneously, I had the privilege of working with relatively new artists of that time, including Tamer Hosny, Hamaki, etc. who have since become household names and were the start of my chart-topping number 1 hits. In addition, one of my greatest signings during my tenure, although it was not a big hit, was the legendary Warda's second last album before she passed away. This was special to me because the artist reminded me of my mother, who was a huge fan. Although I paid a hefty advance for the album, it is something I am personally proud of.

While at EMI Records in Australia, I also had the pleasure of working on Farid Al Atrache's catalogue. My father loved Farid Al Atrache, and just before my father passed away, I remember driving in the car with him, listening to the music that he was so familiar with, yet it was so new to me. I think, in a way, we shared a very special experience. These experiences highlight the profound personal connections between my work and my family, making my accomplishments even more meaningful. "Reflecting on that era, I am grateful for the rich tapestry of talent and creativity that shaped the landscape of Arabic music."

On the international stage, I am blessed to have worked with an amazing mentor in New York. Billy Mann led all A&R efforts globally, showcasing his unique blend of artistic insight and business acumen, stemming from his own background as a real artist. His influence left a lasting impression on me. During this role, I remember he required me to create artist business plans. A particular instance stands out when I was attempting to sign a local artist from the desert. This artist, while relatively unknown globally and lacking a social media presence, had significant local success. When asked about the artist's social media following and website, I replied that he had none. In a humorous yet enlightening moment, the emphasis was placed on the importance of justifying the advance and assessing plans for artists. Though I didn't sign that particular artist, the lesson proved invaluable.

Another person I would like to mention in this book, who is also on the international stage, is Sinan Nergis. He was my business partner from Turkey, and we enjoyed numerous number one hit projects together. For almost three years, nearly everything we released achieved massive sales and hit number one. Sinan truly understood the business where Arabic music meets the West. Our business continues today, even after the EMI Music era, as he has helped me with various key projects including Coke Studio.

Sinan is also an artist in his own right, known not only as a producer but as a pioneer in Arabic fusion. I remember when he would visit me in Dubai, we would arrange interviews for him, as the press was fascinated with his content. Sinan always pushed me to strive further, and he has always been a loyal and dear friend. I owe him a lot of gratitude and love him very much.

"I am fortunate to have played a role in the success of numerous #1 records with various artists and compilations. I remember creating a goal to myself of how many albums can I have in the top 10 at one time, at one time I had 6 out of the top 10, its crazy when I think of this now that I had a game plan of having a minimum of 8 to 10 number 1 albums in each year. This success can be attributed to a culmination of many factors, including great surroundings, an exceptional internal team, dedicated partners, and simply being in the right place at the right time.

I must also acknowledge the invaluable contributions of my external partners, including distribution partners at Viva

Entertainment, Ziad Karimah and Kapany, and retail partners Bassem Said and his team at Virgin Megastores. Additionally, Phillip Riachy at Channel 4 Radio has provided unwavering support that has been instrumental in our success.

I am incredibly fortunate to have built relationships and connections that continue to thrive today. Whether it's my honed DJ skills, developed through a deep understanding of the dancefloor and an obsession with pleasing the audience, or an intrinsic sense of what resonates with people, all these factors have contributed to the creation of commercially successful records."

Leaving EMI Music - The Corporate Life

In late 2011, I made the decision to resign from EMI. Initially planning to return to Australia for a new chapter in life, a turn of events and a strong push from two close friends, Abed and Anis, convinced me to stay in Dubai and open my own business. This decision ultimately led to the formation of my own company, Lionheart and becoming a part owner in a production house named Mindloop studio. I remember Abed said to me you are opening a company and accompanied me during the license process to ensure it happened and a week before this Anis sent me a gift to my house that included a brand new computer, a phone, plant for my office and a high end pen for future contracts, at that time I felt I can't return this I have to set up a business now and I owe so much gratitude to them for this.

Departing from EMI was a moment filled with uncertainty as I stepped away from the corporate world. This is around the time that I became very good friends with and still continue to be with Rania Hamadeh. She is an inspirational woman that I learnt so much from, she would tell me "Richard stop talking so much and be careful of who your real friends are", always giving me wise words and from this we did many successful projects together and developed a trusting friendship relationship, I believe our personalities complimented each other so much, her personality was no fuss, blunt and wise and you knew if she didn't like you and at that time I was more smooth yet errand at times.

Within the same year little did I know that within the same year, I would become the executive producer of The Voice and X Factor, securing a sub-label deal with Sony Music. In reflection, what is crazy is that I was working for both competing companies, Universal Music and Sony Music Entertainment, in an A&R capacity, which is almost unthinkable today. This experience underscored the reality that a single decision can open doors to new opportunities and unforeseen growth. The advice I received from Anis, who was my major inspiration and mentor who is 20 years older than me and is a prominent major successful businessman in Dubai, was amazing. I remember he flew me to Switzerland where we would go for walks and have deep chats, his philosophy was simple yet profound, his metaphor was business can be like a plane taking off and throughout the journey there will be turbulence, he said it's good to know what you want and to adapt to situations as long as you are on your path, it might not be the exact vision after a year and its ok embrace it, he also said surround yourself with great people and people who are smarter than you and finally the secret sauce was that you need to have unwavering faith in Arabic he said Atikil ala Allah, you just never know how things happen with faith, the next opportunity can be around the corner. Anis provided me with the invisible confidence that I can really do this, he believed in me, and it pushed me, I have so much appreciation, respect and gratitude for him and his family.

   During that time of setting up my business I started getting close with another prominent producer and music man from the region named Hadii Sharara, we worked on so many hits together not only for the Voice and X Factor. For me he is the greatest music producer in the modern history of the Arabic pop region, and I still think he is the up there with the best in the west, a talent that is not yet fully exposed. Until then I always thought in my own perception that I had the best ears in the music business and when I met him and started to become close friends, spent time in studios with him, I realized that I met my match if not he was better in different ways. Hadii and I aligned so much being both into funk music of the west and both big Max Martin fans of international pop music. We spent a lot of time together when he visited Dubai or when I was in Beirut and it was always a time of laughter, wisdom and sharing of great music in my convertible blasting songs like "Stayin Alive" or some Stevie Wonder classic. He used to call me golden ears and coming from him is a huge compliment. Today although we don't see each other that often, there is a big mutual respect. I owe a lot of gratitude to Hadii not only in music as he helped me to further educate me better in both genres of Arabic and International music, wiser in the business, Alpha man traits and there are some of my stories in this book that reflect that. He also gave a glimpse into the high life of a celebrity lifestyle, after hanging out with him my whole fashion and appreciation for high quality changed as did my outlook on many things.

      Another person in that time created confidence for me and that was Youssef Dandache, he is a long distance relative from my Jbeil ancestry, he is a staunch loyal guy that is younger than me however ever so wiser than me in many ways, when starting up your own business it's great to have strong guys in your corner that will support you. In a way he was the only extended family I had in Dubai as I had no real relatives there and he was ever so welcoming to me. Whenever I had difficulties or challenges, he helped me so much in getting out of issues personally and in business. At a time whilst juggling 3 TV shows he came in and cleaned so much mess for me on the Voice project. In a way he created a perception at least for me that no one could mess with me and would always tell me to be careful of particular people and help find me opportunities. I appreciate him so much for this and he remains a dear friend and relative. There are a few lessons in this book that he was part of.

My business was thriving until early 2016, when the local conflict in Yemen began to take its toll. Like many other companies, we faced increasing instability, with large sums of outstanding payments affecting our cash flow. This led me to sell my share of Mindloop studios in 2016 at a significant loss, which turned out to be a profound learning experience for me.

While I retained ownership of my other venture, Lionheart company, this marked the beginning of a series of significant personal and professional challenges. About a year later, my then-wife and I separated, further adding to the turmoil.

This is the time I developed a close long-term friendship and business relationship with DJ Bliss, Marwan Al Awadi. I had met Marwan a few years before in my time at EMI Records however during this period in 2016 of uncertainty about my future and whether I should stay in Dubai, I ended up starting a partnership with him in a studio business and became his business manager. I believe we were both very positive influences on each other, and to this day, we have a deep friendship beyond business. He is very inspiring and has become very successful, and I am so proud of him. After all these years, and after I decided to move back to Australia, Marwan remains one of the main reasons to return to Dubai to stay close to him as he is family. I don't think anyone can meet a more special person than him.

Finally, a couple of years before founding Lionheart, I wanted to mention that I rediscovered my passion for DJaying in Dubai. Collaborating with friends Raki Phillips and Alain who organized one-off parties named Jam Dubai and connecting with a booking agent locally, I successfully relaunched my DJing career. By 2017, I found myself performing up to six nights a week in packed venues. Today, Lionheart embodies a fusion of all my passions, offering services ranging from mind fitness to entertainment and business consultancy. I consider myself blessed to have pursued what I love throughout my career, often feeling like my vocation has been a vacation. Working with prominent international brands and artists, my journey has been jam-packed with remarkable experiences.

Through all this, I've come to understand the importance of adaptability and resilience in both business and life.

"Seeds of Manifestation: A Journey from Career Planning to Mentoring Success in Music and Beyond"

As I bring this chapter to a close, I'd like to reflect on the idea that we unconsciously plant seeds for our future, and though nothing is guaranteed, these seeds have the potential to manifest, much like crops in a farmland. I want to touch briefly on the power of manifestation. During my course in 1996, I created a 10-year career plan. I rediscovered it a decade later while cleaning out old paperwork. Remarkably, it stated my goal of becoming a senior music label head by 2006. Mission accomplished.

Upon my initial move to Dubai, I approached it with a determination to prove myself, almost like a cowboy shooting from the hips. In hindsight, my hidden motivation was to prove some doubters in the Australian music industry, personal friends, wrong and eventually return to work in the Australian music industry at the highest level and make a significant impact. However, this vision did not materialize as I had envisioned.

Beyond my love for music, I have always held a keen interest in sports, particularly my team the Blues in Australian Football League (AFL), and the psychology of the mind. Amidst the growth of my DJ career, I dedicated significant effort to mentoring my next-door neighbour, Bachar Houli, who was around 8 years old at the time. We shared a love for our football team Carlton, and he became like a little brother to me. I shared my learnings and motivated him, envisioning that he could become the next big star. I'm proud to say he has indeed become a fine young man, a great role model, and a well-established Australian Rules football star. This early experience aligns with my current work in mental fitness, highlighting the universal principles of personal development that apply whether in football, music, the corporate world, or simply being a good person. I feel blessed to be featured in Bachar's book titled "Faith, Family, and Football," and he is someone I truly admire.

The now and the Future.

As I wrap up this book and pen down these final words in 2024, I find myself wanting to share my knowledge with those I meet in the world, either through this book or in person. This is my story, a story primarily inspired to guide my daughter through her future, whether in great or challenging times. I hope she can use this as a resource to help herself and others through my experiences.

Finalizing this book and re-reading it before it goes to the publisher for distribution has been an amazing opportunity to reflect and understand that I am always navigating through challenging and triumphant periods. I often ponder what lies ahead and grapple with the accompanying anxiety. I acknowledge that, just like everything in life, while you're in a phase, it won't be the last, and it is temporary.

I reflect on the challenges since my wife and I parted in 2017, which have been the most profound for both of us. As you can imagine Dubai is known for the housing rents to be expensive and I was paying for two rents, one for my family and the other for my own accommodation once I left my family home. There have been difficult times in business and life where I had to be extremely careful with my spending and budget. This caused much angst for my ex-wife and me, and it sometimes limited me extremely, including purchasing things when I wanted or my ability to join friends for dinners that were out of my price range. It was a real challenge living in a progressive city like Dubai and our focus and priority was always on ensuring our daughter went to the best schools and had whatever she needed within reason.

Only my close friends, whom I appreciate so much, and they know who they are, including family in Dubai and Melbourne, knew this and understood that I was a man on a mission to provide and to hopefully not burden my daughter so she could focus on school.

This is not to say I excelled in my mission, but I did my best. At times, it felt like the most arduous journey since the loss of my parents. Yet, I remind myself that this, too, shall pass, and I take solace in reflecting on my life's journey.

One thing remains certain: we all require moments of recalibration, focusing on self-healing, and seeking guidance from those capable of assisting. The human body is truly remarkable, providing invaluable feedback. Embracing this feedback and taking actionable steps towards improvement is paramount. With perseverance and dedication, progress is inevitable.

I consider myself fortunate to have a deep connection with God and to receive profound spiritual guidance from various sources that enter my life to aid in my healing journey. Most importantly, I strive to remain inspired, maintain faith, and continually strive to do my best.

However, like many individuals, I occasionally find myself succumbing to negative thoughts when reflecting on the past. I question whether I could have done more, been a better father, brother, husband, cousin, uncle, friend, or colleague. I ponder if perhaps I didn't exert enough effort, if my patience was excessive, or if I failed to attain the desired level of success. While these negative ruminations may appear valid in hindsight, I endeavour to perceive them as opportunities for self-assessment, utilizing them to foster growth, inspiration, and leadership.

I know I did my best, and my life has been dynamic to date, and it will possibly continue to be. I always tried to act ethically and with integrity. I gave a lot, helped many, and stayed true to myself. Some critics might say I was too kind-hearted, while others might call me selfish, or claim I wasn't good at business and missed many opportunities. Everyone has their opinion, but the most important opinion is my own. I'm working hard to keep my mindset focused on the now without dwelling on or regretting the past. As the saying goes, if you keep looking in the rearview mirror while driving, you might crash or never reach your destination.

I feel blessed that I have dear and close friends in my life that inspire me to constantly check in and audit myself,

I don't want to sound too philosophical, but I believe in destiny, and that it's shaped by the decisions and actions we take and that is why it's so important to surround yourself with great people. When I look back at some of the serendipitous events in my life, it feels like magic, or that I've been blessed—perhaps it's good karma for helping others or just simply my journey. In the end, I think of Abraham Lincoln's words: "The best way to predict the future is to create it." or to the best of your ability as in my belief GOD has his plan.

In the last two years I've been fortunate to work in diversity equity and inclusion with Cultural infusion and additionally the soccer business as a director of events and entertainment, cultural attaché for the Australian national soccer team in the Qatar 2022 world cup and additionally I worked as a tour manager in the 2023 women's soccer world cup in Australia.

I have had an amazing experience in the sporting world in which I see the synergy and uncanny similarities between sports and entertainment.

In recent times, I've had the privilege of collaborating with esteemed companies such as Warner Music and Massive Music/ Songtradr as a consultant. Every day, my goal is to impart my experiences to assist and add value—a mantra that guides my life's endeavours. Whether it's discovering talent, nurturing aspiring artists, or aligning brands with music, I remain dedicated to these pursuits.

I feel humbled to have been involved in shaping cultural shifts within the music industry, particularly with the emerging generation of Arabic hip-hop and pop artists. Additionally, I find fulfillment in facilitating connections between brands and music.

I recognize that the landscape of my work is ever evolving; by the time this book is published, it may have already transformed significantly. Despite the challenges inherent in today's era, I embrace the uncertainty and continue to evolve. While some may question whether I still hold the same prominence in the music industry or business, I respond with the acknowledgment that I am constantly learning and adapting. Though I may no longer be the A&R professional in his prime, my mindset has evolved, and I find contentment in this growth.

I am at peace and have no regrets about my decision to move back to Melbourne from Dubai. One day my daughter may ask me again what the reason is and why when we were making more money and arguably a better lifestyle in Dubai. The answer is not simple however this decision was influenced by several factors, including my love and connection with family, schooling and future for my daughter, nature, the love for my football team Carlton (haha) and a desire to be closer to my dear friends. This is not to say that I didn't have close friends and like family in Dubai however it's different and I felt that I still have something to offer back home, and I hope it will one day transpire. In retrospect, I understand why I faced struggles over the past few years—it was challenging to want to return home while having one foot in Dubai and the other in Melbourne.

Dubai offers immense opportunities, and I think, unconsciously, I may have self-sabotaged to avoid taking on too much work there, so I could return to Melbourne and start a new chapter in my life, despite most opportunities coming from the Gulf region. Only time will tell, and I hope I can continue working between the two cities I love.

"I want to emphasize that this is me, and you need to embrace your uniqueness as well. Every lesson, whether learned now or in the future, contributes to the rich tapestry of my journey—a marathon of experiences. Embracing the certainty of uncertainty, I choose to adapt, give my best, and find joy in each moment. Ultimately, this is who I am: Richard Rashid Hussein. And just as I embrace my individuality, you should also be proud of being a unique individual."

Chapter 1: Connected.

In my humble opinion, as a professional DJ performer for over 30 years, here is my take on the essential ingredients for a successful Artist/DJ performance and customer experience. While customer experience is subjective, if the customer attends with the intention to enjoy an event, the following are crucial moving parts:

Mindset of Performers: First and foremost, the performers' mindset plays a pivotal role. They should be able to switch into the confidence zone when the performance starts, believing that, regardless of the event's nature, their performance will be of the highest calibre.

Customer-Centric Focus: The performer's love for being customer-focused ensures a higher probability of success. Whether there is one or a hundred people in the audience, consistency in delivering a high-performance experience is key.

Song Setlist and Preparation: The setlist, preparation, and the ability to adapt during a performance are crucial elements for success. The flow and selection of songs contribute significantly to the overall experience.

Event Factors: Various factors, such as the promoter, location, venue, food, and drinks, contribute to the success of a performance. Additionally, branding, marketing, and communication before and after the event, along with the stage, sound equipment, management, roadies, and audience interaction, all play integral roles.

Ambience and Production: The dance floor, ambience,

production team, lighting, audience, staff, and security are essential components. Even the door person, who may decide who enters or not, contributes to the overall success of the performance.

Music Encore: Finally, the music encore is a critical part of the performance. Each of these factors collectively contributes to a successful performance. Viewing business in a similar light, success is the sum total of many things with numerous moving parts.

Chapter Lesson: The sum total of all these factors may determine success, and imperfection can be beautiful. Live in the moment, enjoy, and adapt. For me, it was always about being positively connected to my trade, selecting positive surrounding environments, and aligning with people who share similar values of professionalism. The movement of all these things is part of the success or failure, and embracing imperfection is key.

Chapter 2: Ice Ice Baby (Alright Stop. Collaborate and Listen.)

In the realm of my professional DJ career, I firmly believe that the true talent lies in the energy you bring and the intentions you project. Various elements contribute to a successful performance, including the calibration with the audience, the flow and speed of songs, selflessness in catering to the audience's desires, and the continual infusion of uniqueness into your set to remain fresh and ahead of the game. Staying at the forefront requires a love for your craft, a commitment to constant improvement, and the ability to bring your A-game when the spotlight is on you. This includes recognizing when a song isn't eliciting the desired response and promptly adjusting.

I've observed that sharing a successful setlist with another DJ might yield different responses, emphasizing the importance of factors such as the energy emitted, song tempo, transitions, and the quality of recordings. Calibration with the audience is akin to establishing a Bluetooth connection, and reading the crowd is the key. Introducing new songs is a skill that involves setting up the room gradually, gauging energy levels, and employing intuitive and micro facial and body reading of the audience.

Similar to the art of romance, timing is crucial. Knowing when to lift or lower the energy is a nuanced skill that requires understanding the dynamics of the crowd. This skill set extends beyond the DJ booth into the realm of the music business, where I applied these principles to introduce new artists and ideas.

Establishing rapport and trust with the audience, strategically slipping in new songs or ideas, and repeating them over time can result in creating a hit within a venue, offering a unique experience that sets you apart.

Chapter Lesson: It's not just about the number of songs or the tools you have; it's about the energy you project, reading the audience through your senses, calibration, trusting your intuition, and adapting. The process is akin to romance: get a feel for the situation, do it from the heart and be open to making mistakes, and know when to make your moves while adapting along the way.

Chapter 3: More Than A Feeling.

      The A & R (Artist & Repertoire) Process: From the demo to the World.

      In the realm of A & R, the journey from a demo to the world is a nuanced process that extends beyond the surface. Just like a DJ must connect with the audience, an A & R professional must look beyond the initial demo quality and presentation, aiming to identify the potential for the next big thing. This process mirrors the DJ metaphor, where the performer plays for the audience while offering a glimpse into personal taste, introducing a song to the world—the dancefloor.

      For me, A & R is about being non-objective, reading the artist beyond what is immediately apparent. It involves a visionary approach, seeing potential success before it fully materializes. The task is akin to sifting through numerous demos, recognizing that some tracks initially overlooked might become hits. Empathy is crucial, understanding that an artist's work is as precious as their own child.

      Selection is the heart of the matter, and it's a complex decision. An artist might possess a great voice but have a poor attitude, or vice versa. Creativity comes into play in finding solutions, such as connecting artists with lyricists if the lyrics are lacking. The A & R process is dynamic, requiring adaptability and the ability to create solutions, much like a DJ responding to the changing audience.

      Finance departments often seek predictions, but the unpredictability of the music business keeps the A & R professional humble. Life constantly introduces unexpected challenges, fostering a hunger for learning and improvement. Despite any individual successes, recognizing the collective effort—internal teams, artists, management, and external factors—is crucial.

In terms of ego, it's a delicate balance. While praise which I received like "golden ears" from legends like Quincy Jones may provide validation, humility is essential. The journey isn't just about liking a song; it involves intangible elements, a fusion of creativity, selection, and everyone playing their role in turning art into a successful business.

Chapter Lesson: The A & R process involves sifting through possibilities, visualizing potential success, embracing creativity, making thoughtful selections, and acknowledging that success is a collective effort. Transforming art into a business is a multifaceted task that goes beyond personal feelings—it's an intricate dance where every element plays a vital role. Study the greats in the business, observe, learn, and implement.

Chapter 4: Don't Stop Believing.

The Artist's Journey: From Thoughts to the Main Stage.

The journey of an artist, from the inception of ideas and passion to the grand stage of adoring fans, resembles a system—an intricate interplay of people, processes, and structure. Having worked with a diverse range of artists, from child prodigies to seasoned performers, I've come to believe that the foundation of an artist's success lies in their thoughts, beliefs, and the environment that surrounds them.

While exceptional talent is a rarity, I firmly believe that every artist's journey begins with unwavering belief and the support system around them, including family, mentors, and guides. Establishing a strong foundation involves surrounding oneself with the right people, from voice coaches to teachers, who can provide valuable direction in the artistic journey. Authenticity is paramount—rather than imitation, artists should draw influences and create their own unique identity.

Having sifted through countless demos, one of the most satisfying aspects of my role was encouraging artists, even in the face of what I might perceive as less-than-ideal music. Witnessing the impact of constructive advice, however small, and observing artists incorporate it into their journey toward success has been truly rewarding. Yet, one of the most challenging aspects remains rejecting someone's music. It's crucial to approach this with positivity, recognizing that opinions are subjective, and the intent is to contribute to the artist's growth.

Chapter Lesson: The artist's journey commences with a thought, fuelled by belief and the right support system. Surrounding oneself with the right people, seeking guidance, and being authentic are foundational. As an A & R professional, encouragement is key, and delivering constructive feedback with honesty and positivity contributes to the artist's evolution. Remember, as an A & R, you're not always right, so approach the journey with humility and an open mind.

Chapter 5: Sweet Child O Mine.

This chapter delves into various facets of the A & R process, encompassing artist development, song licensing, and connecting artists with essential resources. The critical aspect lies in envisioning how a particular song perfectly aligns with an artist, a process less applicable for singer-songwriters who don't rely on external resources.

Reflecting on experiences of visiting writers' and producers' studios, I recall urging them to reveal the hidden drawer of hits. Some songs showcased great intros and verses but lacked in chorus or arrangement, while others lingered in perpetual refinement due to personal attachment. Recognizing the charm in simplicity, a catchy hook, or even a gimmick, my decision to purchase a track often hinged on the writer's emotional connection to the song.

In artist development, the key is establishing an emotional and intellectual connection with the artist, providing them with the necessary tools for growth. This involves introducing them to potential co-writers, producers, or managers. Patience is paramount in this journey, striking a balance between dedicated support and focusing on artists generating business.

Navigating the delicate phase of an artist's early development requires discernment, and while some may argue that it consumed valuable time, I view each experience as a personal learning opportunity. The chapter emphasizes the importance of communication, hustle, and adaptability. Asking the right questions is essential in uncovering potential hits hidden in the secret drawer. Building rapport and understanding the artist's perspective is crucial, recognizing that their art is as delicate as their own child.

Chapter Lesson: Initiate inquiries to unveil potential hits, prioritize rapport and understanding, embrace the hustle, and remain adaptable. Recognize that each person's art is akin to their own baby, demanding delicate handling and care. Finally, be open minded, the demo may not be of your liking however what is important is to be non-objective and ascertain whether there is a potential audience that makes financial sense.

Chapter 6: Come Together (Right now.. over me.)

The role of an A&R/producer often extends to forging strategic alliances among artists, ranging from duets and music collaborations to video productions. These partnerships aim for win-win scenarios, exploring opportunities to enter and expand into new markets. Iconic examples include KD Lang with Tony Bennett and Brandy with Monica. In some cases, influential producers like Quincy Jones, movie directors such as John Landis, and artists like Michael Jackson create partnerships that reshape the music landscape.

This chapter shares a story from 2007, highlighting the impact of last-minute decisions in the music industry. In late 2006, we signed a particular Artist to a record deal, seemingly on the eleventh hour. Initially, I offered an advance for what I believed to be a promising addition to our label's portfolio. After the release, the track gained traction, and an unexpected opportunity arose. A DJ from Holland named DJ Idriss expressed interest in remixing the song, presenting an intriguing concept. Despite reservations about altering an already successful album, I eventually engaged with the persistent DJ.

Collaborating on the idea of adding an English rap to the Arabic song, we developed a demo. Although the artist initially hesitated, I persuaded him to embrace the concept. With a clear vision, I secured additional investment funds for a video and promotional campaign. The re-edition of the album, featuring the new single, proved to be a major success, turning it into a massive hit.

Chapter Lesson: Establishing strategic alliances is crucial for mutually beneficial business endeavours, emphasizing the importance of timing and a willingness to try new concepts. The success of an alliance doesn't always hinge on big names; instead, it may thrive if the content that is unique and exceptional.

Chapter 7: What A Fool Believes, Growth, Relationships.

Following this notable success story, my boss at the record label advised that additional funding approval hinged on securing the artist for future album options. Despite the artist's verbal commitment to a continued partnership without formal contracts, I negotiated persistently with the company. The artist assured me of our collaborative success and future endeavours, but I held firm to add a small option in the contract for an option negotiated in good faith. However, the subsequent year brought an unexpected twist. As he prepared to release his new record, his monumental success, including significant brand deals, attracted my competitor, who offered double the advance. Despite the artist's desire to continue working with me, or what I thought was the case, the allure of a more lucrative deal proved decisive.

In another instance, an aspiring and affluent artist with a substantial budget for his album approached my office. Having invested significantly in collaborations with renowned writers and producers globally, he believed his stardom was inevitable and sought a partnership with me. I candidly expressed my opinion, emphasizing that success in the industry entails more than just financial investment—it requires careful song selection and image cultivation. While the artist believed in his potential, I stood my ground to uphold my principles and declined to sign the album. Subsequently, the album did not achieve the anticipated success.

Chapter Lesson: This chapter underscores the reality of the industry—wins and losses are inevitable. It emphasizes the importance of formal and watertight contracts over verbal assurances and dispels the notion that financial investment alone doesn't guarantees success. It takes more than money alone to make it in the music business especially when establishing a long term and rewarding career.

Chapter 8: When The Going Gets Tough, The Tough Gets Going.

In the midst of promotional activities for one of our latest album releases, we struck a deal with a local promoter to cover travel and accommodation expenses for our visiting artist. The agreement included the artist making a brief appearance at the venue and performing an improvised song, a plan we had discussed and agreed with the artist and manager beforehand.

However, when the time for the appearance arrived after a long day of promotions, the artist surprised us by refusing to sing or even appear. Faced with an awkward situation, I encouraged the artist and manager to honour the commitment, and eventually, he agreed to appear without singing. This unexpected turn of events offered valuable insights into local culture and the dynamics of working with promoters.

Apologizing to the promoter for the unforeseen circumstance, he remained composed, acknowledging that such challenges were inherent in the business—sometimes you win, sometimes you lose. Despite the hiccup, our relationship with the promoter remained intact. However, he had a plan to ensure the artist remembered the incident. The promoter treated the artist exceptionally well, wining and dining him lavishly. When the time for the scheduled song arrived, the artist, appreciating the hospitality, expressed a desire to sing. Excitedly, I relayed this to the promoter, anticipating his agreement. To my surprise, he stood firm and declined, choosing not to grant the artist that pleasure. The promoter stuck to the original plan, leaving the artist wanting.

I conveyed the decision to the artist, who pleaded to change the promoter's mind. However, the promoter stood firm, communicating that he had declined. This experience left a lasting impact on the artist and contributed to the industry's recognition of the promoter's integrity. This unconventional incident highlighted the power of strong decision-making, resisting temptation, and the prospect of delayed gratification.

Chapter Lesson: This chapter underscores the unconventional aspects of the music industry, demonstrating the power of making strong decisions and resisting immediate gratification. It emphasizes that, in the unpredictable world of the music business, maintaining integrity and upholding commitments are essential for long-term success.

Chapter 9: Walk Of Life.

  An artist's journey in the music industry is indeed a walk of life, filled with highs and lows, triumphs, and challenges. Some artists may experience the pinnacle of success, while others face the struggles of financial instability or a decline in popularity. There are complexities and issues below the surface that many people would not know within the entertainment business, some examples are mental and financial health issues to a contrasting example of artists like Toni Braxton who I believe went broke three times.

  The interplay between the left brain (logical) and right brain (creative) aspects of the industry is a fascinating dynamic. Artists must find a balance between creativity and business acumen to thrive. The challenge arises when once-popular artists find themselves in a position where their music no longer sells, requiring them to innovate or make strategic career moves.

  Clive Davis's wisdom underscores the longevity of a music career, citing inspiring stories of comebacks by Rod Stewart and Carlos Santana. The unpredictable nature of the industry means artists may experience unexpected resurgences, similar to fashion brands like Levis, Champion, or Fila.

  I always explore strategies to maintain an artist's integrity, balancing honesty and creative solutions. Creating best-of albums, remixes, and exploring collaborations with emerging artists are avenues explored to revitalize struggling careers.

  The music career journey is inherently filled with highs and lows. Whether an artist's trajectory is swift or gradual, humility is crucial. If I am in a position to offer advice in which I have done with some dwindling stars, the emphasis is on respect, honesty, and problem-solving during tough conversations. Personalizing the journey, being sincere, and approaching challenges with a non-personal perspective contribute to the artist's enduring walk of life in the music industry.

The same examples above can be said about the career of a music executive, we all have highs and lows that is a given and we need great people around us and advice from mentors to help us navigate the walk of life. Success is not linear; it ebbs and flows hence why staying humble is key.

Chapter Lesson: The music career journey mirrors life itself—a series of highs and lows, unpredictable twists, and inevitable challenges. Careers can soar or dwindle swiftly, lacking a linear trajectory. The key is to embrace these fluctuations with humility, recognizing that success is transient.

For those privileged to offer advice, a stance of unwavering respect and smooth communication is paramount. Engaging in tough conversations becomes a necessity, demanding honesty and a proactive approach to problem-solving. Importantly, these interactions should remain non-personal, acknowledging the intrinsic variability of each individual's career path.

Chapter 10: I Did It My Way.

In 2006, during a business trip to Egypt, I encountered a veteran artist with a significant reputation. Despite the artist's long-standing career, I listened to the latest album objectively and found it lacking substance. I had a lot of pressure from our local Egypt office to sign it and to work with this Artist. Choosing to reject the deal with empathy, I faced scepticism from industry peers who doubted my understanding of the market as a Westerner Arab. Despite the decision, I trusted my instincts, maintained my integrity, and it turned out to be not a hit. Five years later, I signed the same artist's albums that proved to be a success, as I found this record to have much more substance.

When I first arrived in the Middle East, my Arabic was almost non-existent—around 10-20 % proficiency at best. According to my own estimate, today it's around 60%. Growing up in Australia, I mostly spoke English, and whenever I tried to speak Arabic, it wasn't very good. One of the major challenges I faced in the Middle East was the language barrier, with its diverse dialects across the Gulf, Levant, and Egypt.

Despite these difficulties, I did my best to learn Arabic, even if it meant picking it up on the fly. For almost a decade, people in the industry would chuckle at my language struggles, yet they appreciated my effort to learn and adapt. As I like to say, "I did it my way." Here are some memorable examples of my Arabic blunders that caused both embarrassment and laughter. Here are some examples,

I asked at a restaurant for freshly squeezed Pepsi Juice, I asked a woman in the bank to throw off her clothes instead of what I meant was for her to throw the paper in the bin. I also told a famous Artist it's a pleasure to NOT meet you and one more for this chapter is that when an Artist told me that her mother was sick, I said in reply God rest her soul instead of I hope she gets better with the will of God. There are many more but for now these are some examples.

Learning a new language, especially one as rich and varied as Arabic, is always a journey. I'm grateful for the patience and good humour of my colleagues and friends who encouraged me along the way. Despite the occasional missteps, these experiences have made my time in the Middle East even more memorable.

Chapter Lesson: Don't be swayed by appearances or history; evaluate based on merit. Trust your instincts, stay true to your principles, and navigate the industry your way. I had a weakness in the Arabic language, yet it became my strength and my uniqueness to stand out.

Chapter 11 Title: Let It Be (there will be an answer.)

In my first year in the Middle East, I recall making a daring move by signing an up-and-coming artist, despite the significant risk involved with a substantial advance. The artist's previous album had not gained much traction, particularly in the Gulf region, primarily finding success in Egypt. The decision to sign this artist transpired during my initial visit to Egypt, where I listened to the final touches of the album with the producer. Witnessing the passion in the producer's eyes and resonating with a couple of songs, I expressed my desire to sign the artist, convinced it would be a major hit album. This encounter marked my introduction to a renowned Egyptian producer, and I believe he appreciated my enthusiasm as a newcomer to the region.

The requested advance was substantial, intended for the artist's investment, presenting a challenge given the artist's limited track record for potential future sales. Despite the significant risk, I persuaded the company with my enthusiasm, ultimately securing the deal. Negotiating with the producer, I structured a step-up deal based on sales, triggering additional advances for added security. I also urged my distributors to take on some risk with potential orders, covering approximately 20% of the potential loss exposure. With determination, we finalized the deal, and I vividly recall my elation at landing the agreement, despite internal scepticism.

Two weeks before the album's release, the Egyptian artist was jailed for failing to fulfill mandatory army service, posing a serious obstacle to promoting the new record. Anticipating a dire situation, I had to devise a strategy to salvage the circumstances however it looked bad, and my CFO let me know about it. To my surprise, the media frenzy, instead of turning negative, generated anticipation and commotion. The artist's fans rallied in support, transforming this setback into an unexpected triumph. Coupled with a stellar record, the album became the biggest of 2006, achieving multi-platinum status and earning me one of my initial accolades.

Chapter Lesson: Find the silver lining in potential disasters, trust in the universe, and sometimes, you just need to "let it be."

Chapter 12: The Show Must Go On.

Negotiation, high pressure, and adapting to seemingly dire situations define the big band story I wish to share. I witnessed a show in front of 25,000 people nearly turning into a disaster, but the frontman adapted masterfully, turning it into a legendary performance. In 2008, Abu Dhabi hosted this band's first-ever show in the Middle East. Unexpectedly, a storm hit—an unusual occurrence in this region. Despite people running for cover, the band continued. The production manager, artist manager, and promoter discussed the possibility of cancelling the show. They even momentarily stopped the band and turned off the sound. The frontman took the initiative, playing acoustic and singing "Singing in the Rain," turning the adversity into a memorable event. As the storm cleared, they resumed the show. As the band's record label, I witnessed deep negotiations and last-minute decisions. Everyone worked selflessly to ensure the show went on.

Another story I would like to share is about a major artist from the USA appearing on a music TV show in Dubai. He was set to perform a new fusion duet with an Arabic artist. We faced major delays because we booked this artist at the last minute after another international artist cancelled about 10 days before the episode shoot. Consequently, we had a small window to finish our local interpretation of one of his big songs. To cut a long story short, we sent the track to him while he was on the plane coming from America.

When he arrived at the studio to shoot his scenes, about two hours before filming, the producer and I sat with him to let him listen to the track. To our surprise, he showed no emotion and asked us to play the song two more times. In the end, he said to us, "My song sounds funny. You cut it up." We responded jokingly, "What do you mean, funny like haha?" to break the tension. Eventually, he said, "You know what, the show must go on. Let's do this," and we did it. 10 years on and this has become one the biggest songs in the region with over 50 million views.

Chapter Lesson: Sometimes plans go sour requiring on the-spot decisions. A potential disaster may hold a silver lining if met with adaptability and teamwork.

Chapter 13: Every Little Thing Is Gonna Be Alright.

How unexpected, assumed disasters can become your biggest hit. In 2013, I was working on a music TV show when a big international Artist cancelled just 10 days before the scheduled performance. She insisted on singing live, which conflicted with our playback requirements. In need of a quick solution, my colleague at Universal Music and I worked tirelessly to reshuffle the talent lineup. We connected a last-minute combination of artists that turned out to be one of the season's big hits. My friend Sinan and business partner from Turkey, with whom I had many previous hits, played a crucial role in this turnaround. Coordinating various elements, from major brands and artists to producers and production, seemed like an impossible task, but we pulled it off. Despite the exhaustion, one key lesson emerged: limited time made us desperate and hindered favourable money negotiations as we had to pay a premium.

I think I could give 100 more examples of how, in the end, everything is going to be alright! The whole book has many examples of this. My philosophy is that in life, things are not done to you, they are done for you. Hopefully, if your intentions are pure and you do your best, everything will turn out as it should. Remember, if you have done your best with the knowledge you have at the moment, then I think you should be OK with that. Some may call it destiny… it's up to you to process this as negative or positive. The choice is yours; I know what my choice is.

Chapter Lesson: Find the silver lining in potential disasters, utilize your network, and don't hesitate to ask for help, even in the most challenging circumstances. When you want something last minute and desperate, expect to pay a premium.

Chapter 14: Don't Leave Me This Way.

On the set of a music TV show I was working on; we had a big artist who wanted to leave after filming for just one hour. She was scheduled to be there for another five hours, and there was a team of about 60 people on set. Stress levels soared as some of the production team came to me to intervene since I had booked her and oversaw the music on set. The artist's manager didn't know what to do. Confronting the situation, I asked, "What is the problem?" The artist replied, "I want to go shopping, and I'll come back later." Knowing that the presenting problem was not the real issue, I stood firm and said, "You are going nowhere; you can't just leave now, and shopping can wait."

I then asked the right questions, negotiated, and discovered the actual problem. Without revealing the personal issue, I addressed it, found a solution, and achieved something close to what was needed. It was not easy, but I managed to make it happen, and we continued the show.

The key takeaway here, which relates to my personal coaching, is that we need to discover what the real problem is, ask the right questions to reveal it, own it and work on an action solution plan.

Chapter Lesson: The presenting problem is not always the real problem.

Chapter 15: Everyone's A Winner.

The power of persuasion and negotiation is a skill where you can win some and lose some. For the music TV show I was working on, we had an artist who did not want to perform if it was not a live performance, although we had stipulated that our show is not live performance oriented. The reason for doing a pre-recorded performance for artists is the associated risks and the lack of appropriate technical equipment. Standing strong, especially after losing one main artist due to the inability to perform live, we had to get creative. Through negotiations, we devised a solution for this artist. We had her sing live in a studio to capture the feel of a live performance and played the live recording as she mimed—ultimately achieving the desired result.

In another story from the year 2000, I was working with Jive Records on the Black and Blue Backstreet Boys tour in Sydney. It was a major tour, with the boys traveling the world in a private plane, covering five continents in five days. I can't recall all the details, but it was a significant world record. I was given the responsibility of taking care of a group of girls who had won a competition to meet the band. It sounded easy enough, so I agreed.

There I was on the private bus with the girls, and as we approached the venue where the band was set to appear, the girls went wild. I couldn't stop them as they ran past me out of the bus, eager to meet the band, causing a commotion. Security had to stop them. I had to gather them all back together and regain control of the situation, which was no easy task.

I spoke to my manager at the time, and he said, "I don't think we can do the meet and greet. They are too wild, and we have a tight schedule." I then had the tough job of informing the girls about this disappointing news. They were devastated. I decided to give it one more try and negotiate the meet and greet. I sat the girls down and explained that I would make this happen, but I was in charge, and they had to remain calm and behave, as we had a very short window to meet the boys.

In a flash, I renegotiated it, and the girls complied and got to meet the boys. In the end, everyone was a winner.

Chapter Lesson: Be creative in finding solutions and adept in negotiations; lessons from past failures can guide your approach.

Chapter 16: Firework.

While preparing for a music production TV show, I faced the challenge of a producer, an artist, and a manager with significant personal issues among them. When the time came for them to collaborate on a song, each individual insisted, "Get him to contact me," resulting in a standoff resembling a game of chess. With no one willing to make the first move, I initiated a three-way conference call, which provided some assistance but didn't fully resolve the issue. Consequently, I took on the role of messenger, coordinating and ensuring that all egos remained intact. Despite the difficulties, we managed to deliver a great product, although the process was a challenging task for myself and my colleague.

During the actual shoot and after the recordings, tensions persisted, leading to a conflict that nearly erupted into a fight at the front of the hotel on the way to the TV set. I remained composed, diffused the situation, and calmed everyone down amidst the yelling and abusive exchanges. Our team worked diligently to conceal the tension, allowing the production to proceed and achieve satisfactory results. However, the experience highlighted the behind-the-scenes challenges that often go unnoticed, showcasing that the music industry is not all fun and games.

Two weeks later, a similar situation arose with another artist. Armed with lessons from the previous incident, I took charge, coordinated key messaging through me, and achieved a much better result.

Chapter Lesson: Your ego is not your amigo; creativity is crucial for solutions and negotiations. Sometimes, you need to take charge and move forward. Understand that in many cases someone's ego is not personal, my philosophy and focus has always been at the work in the moment and to not give energy to a firework ego, if you are patient the fire will subside in due course.

Chapter 17: All I Need Is A Miracle.

Driving into the pyramids with Artists for our TV show shoot, our hire car driver faced a precarious situation when illegal items were discovered in one of the cars that included me and the Artist. This put the record label, brands, artists, and production crew in an embarrassing and dangerous position. To address the issue swiftly, negotiation, honesty, and rapport became crucial.

At the entrance security, sniffer dogs detect something in one of the convoy vehicles, leading to a standstill. With a massive production team and major brands involved, I engaged in fast thinking and negotiations with the local authorities. Initially resistant, the police captain was not swaying, and even a subtle attempt to offer money worsened the situation. Retracting, I proposed allowing the artists to enter and film while addressing the issue separately, a suggestion the captain finally agreed to, relieving the tension.

As the authorities questioned our driver, I represented my team during the interrogation. However, a new challenge arose when an altercation involving one of the artist's friends occurred at the entrance. The heightened vigilance prompted a search of her car, accidentally spilling smoothies and leading to a chaotic confrontation. Balancing multiple challenges, including an upset brand and an artist refusing to film if her friend could not enter, I calmed the situation. Taking the artist to meet the captain, negotiations resumed, resulting in a positive resolution. The captain, content with a memorable picture with the artist, allowed us to proceed with filming, averting a close cancellation.

Meantime after the intense interrogation the driver owned up to him owning the illegal item and they took him away.

Chapter Lesson: Crazy situations demand fast thinking, out-of-the-box ideas, intuition, negotiation skills, and sometimes, a miracle. When your faced with situations like this the true you come out and if you have good values and always look for positive outcomes hopefully you find a sound resolution.

Chapter 18: Superfreak.

While filming a music TV show in Egypt, a seemingly simple request for a diet soda turned into a major on-set issue. Despite multiple attempts to get the drink through the production assistant, the artist's desired beverage was unavailable. In Egypt, it's common to offer a tip for faster service, but even this didn't yield results.

When the production assistant confessed that particular diet soda wasn't readily available, suggesting an energy drink as an alternative, the artist became agitated, leading to a heated confrontation with the production manager. Frustrated with the handling of her request, the artist demanded the immediate firing of the production manager and insisted on removing the manager's name from the show credits.

In an effort to diffuse the situation, I, along with the head of production, decided to tell a little lie. We pretended to fire the production manager for the current episode to appease the artist, assuring her that the production manager would not be back for the next episode. This strategic move successfully calmed the artist, and we were able to resume filming.

Chapter Lesson: Sometimes, a little white lie is necessary to calm a diva, ensuring that the show goes on smoothly.

Chapter 19: Causing A Commotion.

Transitioning from one diva encounter to another, this time at a major regional news and entertainment TV network, I found myself dealing with another memorable challenge. An artist in town had requested a last-minute interview, and despite typically assigning such tasks to my PR/Promotions staff, after his request, I agreed to handle it personally given the artist's preference for dealing with the boss in the Middle East.

Before the live interview, the artist was constantly complaining about various issues, from not being allowed to smoke in the office to delays in hair and makeup. As we approached the interview, approximately 5 minutes before going live, the artist noticed a slight misspelling of his name and wanted to abandon the set. Faced with a live broadcast and prior promotion of the appearance, I had to remain composed and prevent his departure.

In a firm stance, I spoke to the general manager of the TV station about the minor mistake, and a quick plan was devised. The GM brought out the individual responsible for the misspelling to apologize, even offering to fire him on the spot. While the artist declined the firing, the gesture appeased his ego, and he cooled down slightly. However, a new problem arose as he became extremely anxious, stating, "I can't do this!" Just 30 seconds before going live, he declared his intention to leave. I grabbed him, insisted he stay, and pushed him onto the set, making a split-second decision in the moment. Although unconventional and based on instinct, it worked. Once he had the microphone in hand, the artist's demeanour shifted, breaking the tension, and the rest of the show proceeded successfully.

Chapter Lesson: Maintain composure and assertiveness amid a disaster; sometimes, instincts can guide you through the moment.

Chapter 20: Heartbreaker.

In my first year in the Middle East, I signed a young, 16-year-old artist. She showed potential with one semi-hit we released, and she was managed by her parents. As you might expect, this story follows the familiar cliche of parents being more involved and pushier than the artist themselves. With massive expectations, they wanted us to treat their child as if she were a major star.

The father, in particular, would spend hours in my office pushing for their agenda. It became too much, especially when he mentioned selling his property for his daughter's career and the supposed loss of all that money, attempting to guilt-trip me. At that moment, I made the decision to drop this artist from the label and part ways. No amount of effort would satisfy their distorted views. It was a difficult choice, and the artist and family were distraught with my decision. However, it was the right one, as they demanded too much time for the potential return in sales. This experience taught me that, moving forward, I would have to make tough decisions, even if they weren't pleasant.

Chapter Lesson: Set better expectations at the beginning of relationships, maintain firmness throughout, and, when necessary, make the challenging decisions. It's not a popularity contest.

Chapter 21: Upside Down.

Recording in the studio with an artist and facing an 11th-hour decision is always a challenge, especially when working across locations—from Dubai, where the artist and I were based, to Beirut, where our producer worked. Upon arriving at the studio, the artist immediately began complaining about her driver getting lost and insisted it was too early to record, despite it being 8 pm. She seemed accustomed to recording in the early morning. Furthermore, she wanted to smoke in the studio, which was against the rules.

As recording time approached and our studios connected technically, the artist suddenly declared that she didn't want to sing and continued to voice her complaints. Despite my best efforts to persuade her, nothing worked. I tried various approaches, including offering green tea and even suggesting she smoke in the studio. My western approach proved ineffective. At this point, my counterpart producer from Beirut stepped in and told me I was handling it wrong. He insisted on speaking to her, and although I was hesitant due to his fiery nature, I saw no other option, either way we were headed for a disaster.

Handing her the speakerphone, the Beirut producer took charge. He was firm and blunt, asking her, "Who the hell do you think you are, Fairuz?" (referring to the legendary Arab artist). He commanded her to get up and record, warning of a big problem if she didn't comply, her response was yes sir. Understanding the culture, the producer got the desired result. That experience made me realize that everything was upside down compared to what I knew. I never wanted to be in such a situation again and decided then and there to become a hypnotist and study NLP to get a better understanding of psychology.

Chapter Lesson: Your way is not always right; sometimes, unconventional ideas can lead to success. Taking risks for rewards, along with negotiation and understanding local culture, is crucial, even if it seems unconventional.

Chapter 22: "I Gotta Feeling": Ownership of Mistakes.

In my first year in the Middle East, I pursued signing a prominent Lebanese artist set to do a duet with Cheb Khaled, a global star. Upon hearing the demo, I was eager to secure the deal. Negotiations with the manager concluded with an agreed-upon price, albeit a high one. Aware of the potential success, I finalized the deal without consulting the C.F.O in details about the financial implications.

Returning to the office excited about the potential hit record, I faced reality when the C.F.O pointed out that I had exceeded the estimates, risking a financial loss with the proposed advance. Realizing my oversight, I approached the artist's manager, a challenging and somewhat embarrassing task as I aimed to establish myself locally. Surprisingly, the manager was appreciative of my honesty, though I feared the deal was lost.

To my relief, a few days later, I discovered that the manager needed our international exposure, creating a mutual dependency. We renegotiated, and leaving the meeting, I had a feeling the deal was salvageable. In the end, I secured the deal by paying less than half of my initial proposal.

Chapter Lesson: When negotiating, crunch the numbers meticulously. Even if you make a mistake, honesty can prevail. Understand the other party's motivations and trust your instincts—they might guide you in the right direction.

Chapter 23: I'll Be There.: Leadership and Resolve.

Sexual harassment incidents involving my promotions staff and certain artists were not taken lightly. The first instance, involving a B plus level artist, came to light during a press conference. My staff member shared the details, assuring me it was manageable but necessary to inform me. After the conference and as promotional activities concluded for the day, I addressed the issue with the manager and later with the artist. Despite the discomfort, we prioritized respect and integrity, deciding not to work with that artist again.

Another similar situation occurred with a different staff member and artist. Following a confrontation, the artist apologized, attributing the behaviour to alcohol. We chose to continue working together, but the relationship was strained. Upholding integrity in such situations contributed to our reputation as a company with strong values.

Chapter Lesson: Engage in difficult conversations, maintain integrity, and do what is right. Support your staff and team, prioritizing their well-being over business considerations.

Chapter 24: Ain't No Mountain High Enough: Customer Obsession.

In 2006, we faced a significant challenge with a regional radio station partnership. A personal issue between one of my promotions staff and the number two regional radio stations, exacerbated by a music promoter close tie to that radio station, led to the removal of all our content from their platform. Initially unaware of the situation, I took it upon myself to investigate.

Personally, reaching out to the music director and promoter, I arranged a meeting one late evening to understand their perspective. The music promoter and director were initially unwilling to play our songs or meet, but through a friend's intervention, we managed to sit down and discuss the issues. What seemed like an insurmountable problem at first turned into an opportunity to strengthen our partnership.

The key was to listen attentively to their concerns and work toward a solution. The promoter had an issue with my staff member, and I addressed that with my staff and for the music director we eventually decided to provide more exclusive releases to them. We learned that owning up to mistakes and having a more dynamic strategy, involving mixing exclusives and sometimes forgoing them altogether, yielded better results. This experience taught us the importance of customer-centric approaches and adaptability.

Chapter Lesson: Listen to your customer, get the feedback and focus on solutions, and be adaptable in your strategies. Sometimes, tweaking your system can lead to stronger and more fruitful relationships. Do your best to be open even if you are in fault and always put their concerns into prospective. I always try to use the golden rule principle which is treat others as one would want to be treated.

Chapter 25: Let's Dance: Finding Harmony in Business.

Managing a diverse array of egos, be it artists, film directors, producers, or senior executives, resembles the role of a DJ controlling a dance floor. As already mentioned previously, during a music TV shoot, a prominent American artist, expressed dissatisfaction with the remix of the song he was required to perform for our show. Despite the initial panic, he maintained professionalism and delivered a stellar performance. Interestingly, the remixed track later became the biggest hit of the year.

Connecting the chemistry among various stakeholders in a production, akin to a DJ transitioning between songs, proved challenging. Whether selecting duet partners or navigating differing opinions from brands, artists, labels, producers, and film crews, the key was focusing on what I could control. Upholding high ethics, relying on intuition, and following professional guidelines became my guiding principles.

While this approach often worked, there were instances where it fell short. Similar to a DJ playing tracks to a diverse audience, not everyone can be pleased 100 percent of the time. It's crucial to recognize that, in business, as on a dance floor, tastes vary. Sometimes, despite your best efforts, not everyone will resonate with your choices. The important thing is to understand that it's not personal; it's about different preferences. By doing your best and adapting, you create an environment where most people find joy.

Chapter Lesson: Business is akin to a dance floor, and as the DJ, it's essential to navigate and work with what you have. Not everyone will like every decision or song choice, but as long as you do your best, that's what counts. Different tastes are part of the diversity of the audience, and adapting to this diversity is key to success.

Chapter 26: New Rules: Bridging Business Cultures.

In the early stages of my business dealings in Egypt, I embarked on a significant music catalogue renewal deal with one of the region's largest labels. Adopting my Western approach, I initiated the conversation with, "Alright, guys, what do you want, and what are you looking for in terms of price?" However, instead of the anticipated response, I was met with blank faces in the boardroom.

Attempting to navigate the situation, I reiterated my inquiry about their expectations for the advance payment. I presented our financial numbers, emphasizing our past collaborations, and expressed my eagerness to renew the contract. Despite my efforts, the boardroom remained stoic, with faint smiles.

It became evident that my Western approach wasn't resonating. What I needed was an Eastern approach, one cantered on building trust through shared experiences, like having a meal together, smoking shisha and engaging in personal conversations.

Chapter Lesson: Understanding the local market and business culture is crucial. Your familiar approach may not always yield the desired results, so be flexible. Tailor your strategy to meet the needs and expectations of your counterparts, and success will follow.

Chapter 27: Price Tag: Upholding Integrity.

In the realm of the music industry, I encountered numerous instances where under-the-table deals were extended to me as a representative of the label. On one occasion, I was offered a substantial sum of 50k, coupled with a 300k investment, to sign an unknown artist. Managers, too, approached me with propositions to inflate deal prices, allowing for a covert cut, assuring that no one would be the wiser.

Despite the allure of quick personal gains, I staunchly dismissed these propositions. Upholding ethical standards and preserving my integrity were non-negotiable. This principled stance earned me ridicule from some industry peers who deemed me overly honest, perhaps even questioning my business acumen for rejecting side money. However, I prioritized building a reputation as an individual impervious to compromise.

In retrospect, friends in the business who engaged inside deals faced varying fates. Some profited and continued unscathed, while others, exposed for their dealings, experienced shorter-lived careers. I, however, remained steadfast in my commitment to avoid monetary side deals, safeguarding the integrity of the international company I represented.

Another example involved an artist who had been signed a few years before my tenure, and while his music had moderate sales on our catalogue, it wasn't exceptionally successful. He requested a meeting with me to discuss regaining his rights. In his contract, there was an automatic extension clause that kept his catalogue with my company for another 5 years. Despite this, he expressed a strong desire to part ways and reclaim his master rights.

I advocated for returning his rights within the company, telling him that if he no longer wanted to be associated with us, I would revert his rights to him. In summary, we successfully reverted his rights, and we went on to collaborate on new and prosperous projects. He later contributed to mixing my local Ministry of Sound compilations, and a couple of years down the line, he became my business partner in a studio.

Chapter Lesson: For me, integrity and reputation trump immediate financial gains. In the long run, these principles contribute to genuine wealth.

Chapter 28: Crazy: Think outside the box, you just never know.

Discussing missed opportunities is never an easy task, as we've all encountered such moments in our lives. Allow me to share an experience involving the "Gangnam Style" track, illustrating how even the most seemingly absurd ideas can become monumental. In 2012, a contact of mine in London urged me to consider licensing this catchy Korean song for the Middle East. My first question was "what language is it in?" He said Korean, and I replied that I can't sell Korean in the Middle East. The proposition sounded weird, and, without delving further, I failed to follow up to receive a copy to listen to. Unfortunately, I later discovered that it became the world's biggest song for that year. Sometimes, opportunities slip through the cracks.

In another story, there was an artist in Egypt who always wanted me to sign him. Most times, when I visited Cairo on business, he would try to get people to arrange a meeting with me or he would run into me randomly in a studio or hotel. I could see a little talent in him; however, I never thought he would become a big star one day. This artist was so pushy that I always tried to avoid him. Fast forward 12 years, and he is now a big star in the region. Before you think it, yes you never know... In my line of business, we are experts, but you never know someone's divine destiny.

Here is another crazy story, back in 2009, I was feeling pretty disenchanted with EMI and started hunting for a new gig. That's when I stumbled across a job opening at a relatively new media company, and the description really caught my eye. But instead of going the usual route and applying like everyone else, I decided to get a little creative. I figured out an angle where this media company could benefit from working with my current employer, and next thing you know, I had a meeting set up with their CEO. Yup, I got him to come to my office to tell me all about his company and he even chatted about the role he was trying to fill. Little did he know, this was my secret job interview. Only this time, I was the one deciding if they were a fit for me. By the end of the meeting, I knew this wasn't the company for me. But hey, it was a pretty creative way to scope things out without putting myself on the line!

Chapter Lesson: No idea is too outlandish; you just don't know what can happen. Embracing the unexpected and fostering a paradigm shift can lead to unforeseen successes. Anything is possible when we remain open to unconventional possibilities. Also, someone's destiny is out of your control, whatever is written for that person is written, this is my belief. We all have hands in things, or we think we do however what is meant to be will always be.

Chapter 29: Invisible Touch: Lessons from a misjudged Album.

In 2007, I signed a sex symbol artist whose previous album had been a massive hit, known for provocative dancing and gimmicks—a genre commonly referred to in the industry as bubble-gum music. Excitement filled the air as I met with the producer in his Zamalek apartment in Cairo, Egypt, listening to the new content that was still in the works. The material was groundbreaking and of exceptional quality, and I was convinced that we were on the verge of creating history. Returning to Dubai, I placed a significant bet on her next album, envisioning that a shift towards more serious, conservative content would captivate audiences. I paid a massive advance, expecting triumphant success. However, the reality was starkly different.

To cut a long story short, the album barely broke even and fell short of expectations. Despite my efforts in retail, radio promotions, and more, it flopped. While I still believe it's a great record, the critical lesson emerged: the disconnect between the music's quality and the artist's image and positioning. Delays in releasing music videos, conflicts between the artist and producer, and misjudgement of our audience compounded the issue. People preferred the artist's old image of sexy and cheeky, rejecting her as a serious artist, regardless of the quality of the content.

In hindsight, this experience led me to reevaluate my approach to selecting and releasing hits. It underscored the importance of understanding the audience, especially when entering new territories. The mishaps and excuses highlighted the elusive nature of success, akin to an invisible touch, controlled by forces beyond our immediate control.

Chapter Lesson: Avoid getting caught up in the hype, know your audience intimately, and recognize that success often lies in the hands of an invisible touch that transcends our immediate efforts.

Chapter 30: Hotel California: Lessons from Rockstar Antics.

"Welcome to the Hotel California, what a nice surprise..." Hotel rooms and artists—surely, you've heard the stories. Here's one: after hosting an artist in town for a music TV show I was working on, they pulled a royal rockstar move, leaving the room in deplorable condition. Stained couches, wine-drenched curtains, broken glasses, and damaged bathroom tiles painted a picture of their outrageous actions. The company had to foot the bill for the damages, a cost often associated with the antics of stars.

Upon discovering the aftermath, my colleague and I addressed the issue with the artist's manager, expressing our disappointment and emphasizing the unacceptable nature of their actions. While we didn't turn it into a massive confrontation, I made it clear that such behaviour was not acceptable. This time, we let it pass with a firm warning.

That same artist's trip led to a big, successful record; however, it was non-stop issues and challenges daily with her and the large convoy that came with her. We had to extinguish problems constantly, including punctuality and dramas.

Chapter Lesson: In the world of artists and entertainment, unexpected issues may arise, and sometimes you have to bear the costs. However, it's crucial to remain firm in communicating boundaries and expectations, even in the face of rockstar antics.

Chapter 31: With a Little Help from My Friends: Navigating Retail Challenges.

In the realm of retail partnerships, maintaining a strong relationship with key players is paramount. I cherished a fruitful association with prominent retailers, meeting them regularly to discuss business. Our agreement involved prime exposure advertising for our new album releases, featuring large posters and eye-catching displays—an effective strategy at a reasonable cost. However, this landscape shifted when a competitor swooped in, paying double for the coveted space. Subsequently, companies with more substantial profit margins outbid us tenfold.

While this setback could have been disheartening, we chose a different path. Rather than lamenting the loss of space, we focused on creative internal strategies. Boosting in-store promotions and incentivizing retail staff through competitions and exclusive events, we made them an integral part of our music discovery journey. Additionally, we supplied them with DJ style curated playlists, actively listening to their feedback. Despite not owning the advertising space, our influence inside the retail environment gained significant traction.

In a separate challenge with the same major retailer, we faced resistance from the main product buyer in their office. Despite our best efforts to build a positive relationship, this individual remained stubborn and unyielding. Instead of persisting with unsuccessful direct approaches, we strategized differently. By engaging with his team and fostering support from within, we turned the situation around. His team, aligned with our products, became advocates, enabling us to navigate the challenge successfully.

Chapter Lesson: In the face of retail challenges, creative and adaptable strategies are essential. Building relationships, involving partners, and actively seeking feedback can open alternative pathways to success. If one door remains closed, explore other doors to reach your destination.

Chapter 32: Everybody Hurts: Navigating Product Placement Pitfalls.

In pursuit of additional funding to support artists, we struck a deal with a brand for product placement in a music video featuring a car brand. While such arrangements had been part of our strategy over the years, this particular instance unfolded as a rookie mistake. In our eagerness, we allowed the brand to feature prominently, occupying more than 60 percent of the video.

The repercussions became apparent upon release. Some TV stations refused to air the song, categorizing it as an advertisement rather than a music video. Recognizing the oversight, we engaged in tough negotiations to re-edit the video. Unfortunately, the brand manager resisted, and by the time we reached an agreement, momentum had waned, leaving both the artist and us dissatisfied.

This experience prompted a crucial lesson for the future. We vowed to approach product placement more strategically, ensuring that brands felt like integral props rather than overpowering elements in the video. This adjustment aimed to prevent any future challenges or questions about the nature of the content.

Chapter Lesson: Embrace mistakes as opportunities to learn and refine strategies. Exercise caution when seeking funds, ensuring that agreements are pre-framed to avoid setbacks that benefit no one in the end.

Chapter 33: It's Not Over Yet: Adapting to Shifting Perception.

Upon my arrival in Dubai and while working for the label, I held onto my passion for DJing from my time in Australia. In Australia, being a DJ not only granted me credibility in the music industry but also provided invaluable insights into dancefloor dynamics, direct feedback on songs, and a keen sense of emerging trends.

However, in the Middle East during that period, being a DJ carried a somewhat negative stigma. I vividly recall encountering sceptical looks from industry professionals when I mentioned my DJ background. One person even took me aside to express that being a DJ didn't project the image of a serious businessman capable of dealing with high-level artist managers.

Initially, I shrugged off such comments, but as time passed, I recognized the potential impact on my business. To safeguard my professional image, I made the strategic decision to downplay my identity as a DJ and ceased performing for a few years. This choice seemed to align better with the prevailing perceptions.

Later in my career, as DJaying gained acceptance and became a cooler pursuit in the region, I reintegrated it into my professional identity. By then, having already established a solid reputation in the business world, I navigated the evolving landscape with confidence.

Chapter Lesson: Understand the dynamics of your market, recognizing that perceptions and acceptance can vary in different regions and countries. Adapt to shifting cultural and professional landscapes, we all have different perceptions and maps of the world of the way we see things, it is important to make strategic choices to align with evolving norms in your industry and territory.

Chapter 34: Walk Like an Egyptian: Navigating Egypt's Business Culture.

In my extensive business dealings across Egypt over 20 visits, I've accumulated a wealth of amusing anecdotes. Often hailed as the Hollywood of the Middle East, Egypt boasts a vibrant entertainment scene, particularly in cinema and music. With its substantial population and a plethora of creatives, Egypt emerged as a hub for music creation, featuring numerous recording studios.

Early in my career, I discerned distinct roles for different regions in the music business. Egypt stood out for music creation, Lebanon for crafting artists' images and music videos, and the Gulf for sales. Despite Egypt's substantial population of approximately 100 million, piracy heavily impacted the market, influencing the regional dynamics.

Adjusting to the local culture posed an initial challenge. Punctuality, or the lack thereof, initially bothered me. Scheduled meetings for 8 pm often unfolded closer to midnight. Messages claiming imminent arrival, such as "I'm on the way" or "crossing the bridge," became familiar refrains, exacerbated by Cairo's notorious traffic. Moreover, business discussions frequently extended from 10 pm to 8 am.

Over time, I learned to embrace the idiosyncrasies of Egypt's business culture. What I initially perceived as disrespect transformed into an appreciation for a unique rhythm. Late-night meetings became the norm, and I grew fond of the distinctive blend of challenge and enjoyment that Egypt offered.

I remember a moment in 2014 when I was working on a project in Egypt for a multinational brand involving two prominent artists, one from Egypt and the other from the UAE. Despite thorough preparation, challenges were a constant companion. On this occasion, we were filming at the Children's Cancer Centre in Cairo, and I had ensured the band arrived at least 3 hours before shooting the artists' duet.

As the band started setting up, I noticed a crucial element missing – the drum set. To my surprise, I inquired about the drummer and the kit. The band leader's response was that he was on his way. Unfortunately, the drummer never showed up, and we were provided with various excuses, ranging from a broken-down car to the promise of buying a drum kit nearby. Approximately 30 minutes before filming, the director and subsequently the brand representatives asked about the drums, putting us in an embarrassing situation.

Faced with Artists waiting and the eager anticipation of the beautiful children from the cancer centre, we had to act quickly. At that moment, I chose honesty and admitted that we had no drums. We worked on an imperfect but functional solution – we decided to do a playback of the recording and not show the drums in the video. Despite the challenges, we pulled it off, turning a potential disaster into a successful production.

Chapter Lesson: Understanding and accepting the local business culture is essential. Embrace the nuances, refrain from taking things personally, and relish the distinct journey each market presents. There is always a solution even if it's not ideal, make do with what you have.

Chapter 35: Another One Bites the Dust: Navigating the Ethical Borders.

During a period when my influence in the music industry was substantial, I engaged in shrewd business dealings that occasionally tiptoed along the border of ethics to secure the best outcomes for my label. A crucial accomplice in these ventures was a partner in Saudi Arabia. Reflecting on those days, we now chuckle at our tag—the music duo—earned through a string of major hits. Our dominance in the Gulf region was so profound that we genuinely believed we held the power to shape or break careers, and, in truth, in some cases we did.

Frequently, we encountered situations where a prominent artist sought to secure a deal for their album, navigating potential labels in the process. Despite our representing labels being the two major entities in the region, we occasionally found ourselves viewed as competitors in the broader market. My label, accompanied by my partner's distribution prowess, formed a potent alliance. In a straightforward manner, we strategized and determined who would acquire the album, subsequently sharing the profits equitably. At times, I assumed the label role, with my partner handling distribution, leveraging the distinctive strengths of our respective companies for mutual profit, occasionally encountering losses.

Maintaining a foundation of trust was paramount. We meticulously balanced our strategic alliance, ensuring that the integrity of our companies remained intact. In instances where a deal offered marginal benefits to our bottom lines, we opted to pass, grounded in professional or personal considerations. 99 percent of the time, it was me getting the label deal, and together we navigated the industry's ethical borders, showing how, despite the challenges, "Another One Bites the Dust" became a fitting nickname for our journey. We decided on the fair price we should offer, keeping integrity for our companies. However, at times, if there was an average deal on the table with not much to gain for our companies' bottom line, we would agree to pass on signing it for a number of professional or personal reasons.

Chapter Lesson: Forge strategic alliances for collective power and shared business success, always mindful of maintaining integrity and ethical considerations.

Chapter 36: Respect.

    Having great relationships and success in the business can provide you with many valuable perks. When we promoted an artist or compilation, I was fortunate to have outstanding partners in (DSPs) digital service providers, radio, print, or retail who supported me wholeheartedly. On the radio airwaves, I could get our music played over 10 times a day if needed and even more. Their loyalty protected us, creating a strong support network. I recall an instance when, out of respect, one artist's entire content was removed from the radio for weeks. This caused a stir in the industry and affected the competitive label and artist. The reason behind this was that the artist I had developed went to a competitor, and it was perceived as a display of disrespect.

    There were times when the support we received from retail, radio, DSPs, and other media felt like a true alliance, akin to a mafia. However, it wasn't a mafia; it was built on respect, and that's what I cherish about the Middle East region.

    Here is another example of the importance of respect that I learned in the Middle East. As mentioned earlier in the chapter, I had an artist walk out of a film set, causing us significant headaches. Later that evening, the artist and their team went out for dinner, and the manager extended an invitation for the evening. Although I was inclined to attend, my friend, the producer, advised against it. The explanation was that since they didn't show respect on the set, and the artist never apologized or personally invited us, we shouldn't grant them the pleasure of our attendance. In the end, we chose not to go. Regardless of whether this decision was right or wrong, I subscribe to and understand the importance of respect.

Chapter Lesson: Respect is earned by giving respect and building a reputation. This can open numerous opportunities and help set clear boundaries in the wider music business ecosystem.

Chapter 37: Gold

In 2009, a unique album landed on my desk, courtesy of a mutual friend of an artist I was on the verge of signing. The album, a captivating blend of classical and world music with electronic elements, belonged to a local Dubai artist. Intrigued, I invited her to my office. As our conversation delved into her vision, I discovered her desire to shun personal fame and focus solely on promoting the music. This marked the first time I signed and promoted an artist without incorporating her image, music videos, or face-to-face interviews.

We navigated this unconventional approach creatively, focusing on aspects like packaging and retail strategy. Upon release, we initiated various campaigns and competitions with our retail partners. The response was swift and promising. Starting within the top 20, the album gained momentum, eventually reaching the pinnacle at #1. Its massive success earned us a Gold record, a testament to outstanding sales in the region. Retailers embraced it wholeheartedly, and its uniqueness resonated with customers. As the songs played in stores, audiences were compelled to buy, fostering a ripple effect as satisfied customers recommended it to others. The album became a timeless classic, and the anticipation for the follow-up resulted in another success.

Beyond the professional success, these releases forged enduring friendships with Hana and her family, a relationship for which I am truly grateful. The experience also imparted valuable lessons about the continual learning journey in business.

Chapter Lesson: Embrace creativity and watch as small victories transform into significant achievements including a GOLD certified record. Your innovative endeavours can lead to lasting friendships and successes that stand the test of time.

Chapter 38: Faith.

In late 2010, a demo album reached my desk, promising rich and unique content. Upon arranging a meeting, I was surprised when an 81-year-old woman and her daughter walked into my office. To my astonishment, the elderly woman was the artist behind the music. She candidly remarked that most of the artists featured on my office posters were rather less than average. It was a first for me to hear something like this, and her words compelled me to listen more attentively. This artist, a renowned painter from Iraq, had transitioned to music when her hands could no longer create art. Intrigued by her story and concept, I decided to have faith and sign her.

However, I grappled with reservations. Would she be the oldest person in history to sign a major record deal? What would my peers and the industry say? Had I lost my sense of direction? Despite these concerns, I trusted my gut feeling and moved forward. Creativity took centre stage, and we decided to feature one of her most famous paintings as the CD artwork. The booklet opened to reveal more of her artworks. To amplify the uniqueness, we planned the album launch in an art gallery, showcasing her timeless art alongside her music. This concept garnered attention from major news channels like CNN and BBC, both eager to run a news story.

As we geared up for the early 2011 launch, the Arab Spring took precedence, diverting attention away from our project. Even the news channels shifted focus due to the regional developments. Undeterred, we released the album titled "Rhythms from Arabia," giving it our best effort and achieving relative success. This remains one of my favourite releases and stories.

Chapter Lesson: Anticipate the unexpected; some ideas may seem crazy initially but can flourish with a leap of faith. By embracing creativity, you can turn nothing into something extraordinary. Recognize that factors beyond your control, such as the political environment, are not personal; simply do your best in the given circumstances.

Chapter 39: Never Gonna Give You Up.

Having worked on numerous releases over the years, I've learned that what I perceive as great doesn't guarantee a hit. This analogy holds true in the DJ world as well. I might believe a song will set the dance floor on fire, but the outcome is unpredictable. While my experience and taste enhance the probability, readiness to adapt is crucial. It involves closely monitoring the audience's reaction and striving to serve them best. Yet, the ultimate result remains uncertain, reinforcing my mindset to never give up.

One of my cherished projects was a collaboration with a renowned regional hit producer, featuring a French African artist and an Egyptian band. I find the track remarkable, and we even released it on vinyl. However, when comparing YouTube views to other releases, this particular song falls short. This aspect is what I love about my work—everything is subjective. Every time I thought I had it all figured out, life presented challenges, bringing me back to reality. Such experiences embody constant learning in life.

Chapter Lesson: For every success, there is an equal, if not greater, amount of failure on the journey. Life offers lessons daily, visible for those who listen and observe. It's about interpreting these lessons, understanding their significance, and embracing continuous learning. Never give up.

Chapter 40: The Time of My Life.

These forty stories offer a glimpse into the behind the scenes of the music business and my life in the realms of both mind and music. Since 2015, I've embarked on a professional journey, blending mind fitness coaching with entertainment. Today, I continue to find joy in my work in the entertainment industry, fuelled by my two passions. Amidst significant challenges, including the loss of both parents within three months during my twenties, I've come to appreciate life more deeply and try my best to use the Arabic word alhamdulillah (gratitude) for everything. Adversity and triumph have moulded me into a stronger individual and made me more spiritually connected and when we are spiritually connected, I believe I am at my best.

Having the time of my life doesn't negate the major challenges. The lessons from loss have instilled in me a commitment to being the best version of myself. Whether as a father, brother, uncle, or friend, my focus is on being a better human being. Success is never guaranteed, but I draw inspiration from my own experience and timeless principles experienced within books with great education that have endured for centuries. Learning is a constant process—be it from sports, global events, or encounters with individuals in various walks of life. The lessons are omnipresent; one just needs to be receptive to life's rich teachings and strive for a positive mindset. Ideally, we should all do what we love and dance to the beat of our own rhythm, finding fulfillment in the process.

Chapter Lesson: Reflecting on all of the chapters above, wholeheartedly do your best and do it ethically, you live one life so make it the time of your life. You will make mistakes on the way and that is the beauty of life and continuous learning. I released this book with so many mistakes and it could be looked at as a rookie mistake. I have spelling and grammar mistakes and decided to reissue another version of this book to remove as much mistakes as possible. I am sure there are still some more mistakes however ill always give my best shot.

All right... let's do one more story... Encore Chapter: "Unbelievable"

In the wild west or the Middle East, a traditional market isn't always conventional; it comes with its unique set of challenges. In a specific country, which I won't disclose, in 2006 we encountered issues releasing content due to the Ministry of Information blocking key releases, including those of Katy Perry and Madonna. While some restrictions were understandable, such as for Katy Perry's "I Kissed a Girl," given the region's conservatism, we had to create special packaging versions for this country, including censoring certain body parts. However, other releases faced unjustifiable blocks, resulting in a significant backlog of unreleased albums that, in my opinion, raised no concerns.

Our distributor suggested a peculiar solution to clear the obstacles and open the doors: payola. The first request was giving a gift and I obliged by sending a brand-new mobile phone, however 3 months later I got a request for another gift and the request was astounding—they wanted a sheep, yes, a literal sheep. Now, try explaining to your accounts department that we need to make such a payment for future business. It was not easy; my local accounts suggested I ask our regional boss in London. All I can remember is him saying, "Can you repeat your request?" while having me on speakerphone and giggling, with some of his colleagues listening in. Sometimes, there are no rules. I went ahead, claimed it as miscellaneous, and, in an instant, we got more releases out.

Chapter Lesson: Expect the unexpected and be prepared to throw out the rule book when necessary. In the unpredictable landscape of the music business, unconventional solutions may be the key to overcoming unique challenges.

Album Credits and Thank You.

This album is dedicated to my beautiful daughter, Sarah M. Hussein. She is an extraordinary girl, a passionate person, music lover, and an artist in her own right. Her birth transformed my perspective on life, and the changes it inspired me in life have been nothing short of amazing. During my wife Dana's pregnancy, I would place headphones playing songs on her pregnant stomach, hoping to give our child an early music fix. From her early years to her teens, I made sure she was exposed to the best music from the Bee Gees and ABBA to the Beatles and various chill-out tunes. Today, as a teenager, she boasts a keen ear for music, and she believes she's surpassed my musical prowess. I'm delighted to pass the mantle to her in our family.

Special thanks to Sarah's mother, Dana, for being an unbelievable support during challenging times and providing invaluable advice with her emotional intelligence.

Peter Barber: Thank you for the guidance, for helping me create a model, and for collaborating on the idea to write this book. I've learned immensely from you, and you are a star! Special thanks to Anjali and Georgia for helping to make this book into reality.

Throughout my journey, I've had the privilege of learning from great mentors in academics and the music business. Though too numerous to name specifically, my gratitude extends to Dr. Anthony Lowe, Dr. Stephen Downes, Martin Comte, David Forrest throughout University.

I would like to give special thanks to all in the below list that somehow have been part of my journey, and this is not in order of appreciation.

DJ's Sharif Galal, Dale, Herc, Megalo, Fady, Vito, DJ's Carlos and Oscar Torero, venue managers/owners Joey & Mark Gualtieri and family, George and Sam Frantzeskos, Terry O'malley, Vlad Genev, Maurits. Record company executives, managers, promoters, and more, I know I have forgotten some. In my early days in the Australian music industry, the entire team at BMG, Zomba/Jive Records, and EMI played pivotal roles. Special mentions go to Paul Paoleilo, Scott Murphy, Tony Smith, Matt Knipe, Con Frantzeskos, Karl Richter, Damian Slevison, Stu Harvey, Will Heine, Follach, Andrea Makris, Suzanne DeSilva, Sarah P, Jered, Sally Power, Connie B, Chelsea Athon, Anthony Boom, Stuart Watson, Martin Dodd. Other industry friends John Scott, Baydr Strik, Michael Gudinski (R.I.P), Michael Chugg, Michael Parisi, Gabby Columbia, Di Torrasian, Ben Pritcher, Gary Henshke, Alf and Nell Cox (R.I.P.) Frank Varrasso, Glenn Dickie, Tony Ishak, Simone Redman, Joey Nemer, John Tripodi for their direct or indirect mentorship and faith in my journey.

The move to Dubai opened doors to work with the best in the business, including locally and internationally. At EMI Arabia, leaders and mentors like Adrian Cheesley, Pascal Galliot, and others dear friends that helped shape my professional growth which I grateful for, I am sure I have missed out on some names therefore I will run some names from the top of my mind starting with the EMI and Universal team and to my Dubai and Middle east peeps, Rania, TD, Hadii Sharara, Patrick Boulos, VT, Naveen (R.I.P),

Stefanie, Raffael, Claudius, Sabine, Dergham Al Owainati, Sunil, Lulla, Raby Hamza, Bashar Sultan, Nolla Azar, Deen, Rachel Monk, Emma Zerbib, Emily, Mario Chourei, Beirut office Joe and Hubert. Notable figures like Mohsen and Mostafa Gaber, Hisham Gazzer, Ahmed Desouki, Nasr and Amira Mahrous, Ali and Samir Mawla, Anas Nasri, Hisham Tawfik, Ahmed Moussa (R.I.P) Mahmoud Moussa, Nassif Kauzman, Ken Pederson (R.I.P.) Peter Bezzano, Sat Basila, Ziad Karimeh, Hassan Taleb, Walid Abou Farhat, Ghassan Ajou, Reem Arab, Ghassan Saad, Oscar D, Phillip Riachy, Myriam music team, Jad Kiwan, Adnan Al Obthany, Prakash and Kapany, Luiza and Christina Formenius, Nikeisha and Jessica Anderson, Richard Crossley, Tarek Arian, Bilal Al Zain, Ghassan Chartouni, Haythem Zayyed, Michael Fadel, Awad El Roumy, Richard El Hajj, Eddie Jazzer, Kevin, Nikola Nakhla Saade, Elie Attieh, Said Mrad, Ralph Khoury, Elie Barber, Guy Manoukian, Moe Hamza, Najdat, Minshawi, Ahmad Ghannoum, Jawad Hashem, Elie Afif, Noor Dagher, Layal Moukahal, Nada Safa, Ramzi Fares. Hashem Zaini, Spek, Fahad Al Hababi, Mardo El Noor, Mo Kubba, Amr Mostafa. Tarek Abdullah, Gamal Marwan, Elie Khoury, ARAD, Raki Phillips, Walid Toufic, Hady Hajjar, Joelle Khoury, Amin Aby Yaghi, Ziad Hamza, Ziad Karima, Kapany, Danny Neville, Rocky Mental, Khalil Chucri, Walid Massih, Shelly Frost, Jean Mouwad, Jean Marie Riachy, Bashar Jawhari, Mohammed and Ilham Madfai, Jean Saliba (R.I.P), Dr Sharif Sabri, Husam Halima, Bilal Dayani. Yasser Hasanan, DJ Idriss, Furad Qaddouri, Tarek Tawakol, Rami Sabri, Dj Kaboo, Ghady Sharara, Hamdi Badr, Yasser Khalil, Robert Fakhri, Bassam Turk, Yasser Nawar, Minshawi, Andreas Konstantinidis, Liliana Abudalo, Lisa Hugo, Marwan Rahbani, Elias Rahbani (R.I.P),

Pierre Achkar, Khodr Alama, Saeed Saeed, Tamir Ali, Elia Mswir, Layla K, Kris Fade, Islam Desouki, Dolly Saidy, Osama Awadi, Emma and Russell, Nadina and Brent, Eve and Brent, Steve Smith and Elissa, and many more who have contributed significantly to my journey. To the Sony music MENA team Charmaine, Craig, Bonnie, Arun and Anna George, Australia team Dennis Handlin, Anthony Smith & Hayden Bell. Finally to the Warner music peeps and Artists from the MENA region, USA and Australia thank you Karima, Ahmed, Alfonso, Tarek, Wisal, Khaled, Noura, Pauline, Cèline, Chady and the M.E.N.A team, Marwan Alsayed in Saudi Arabia and in North America Global, Joshua, Kylee, Selena, Bello and the local team in Australia Mo Komba, Dan Rosen, Ben and Julian Schweiter.

To the team at massivemusic/SongsTradr Pierre and Julia in Dubai, it's a pleasure. Thanks to the Cultural infusion team Melbourne Peter Mousaferiadis who I have known since I was a kid and has always supported me.

I had the pleasure of working with or meeting major International music business players such as Miles Copeland, Quincy Jones, RedOne, Zak Dekkaki, Luis Medina and Abed Hager (R.I.P), Mario Reyes, Peter Lopez (R.I.P.), Nile Rodgers, Farid Nasser, Madeline Nelson, Billy Mann, Benton and Christle James, Jerry Wonder, Wassim Saliba, Massari, Wyclef Jean, Ashish, Leslie Braithwaite, Jermaine Jackson, Costi, Noval BeatGeek, Erik Lewander, Khalid Schröder, Kool and the Gang, Will Smith, Eric Madrid and others. Their influence and collaboration have left an indelible mark on my career.

I'd like to also thank the numerous Artists I had the pleasure of working with over the journey some have been mentioned earlier in the thanks, however there are too many to mention, our friendship, experiences and musicianship has somehow helped shape me to become who I am today.

Special thanks to my parents, big sisters and husbands, real sister Nada, Rita Rashid, who introduced me to music and taught me some valuable life lessons. Deepest gratitude also goes to Khol Houli, my big brother and mentor, the person who constantly keeps me grounded and perhaps I have most love for and have my deepest appreciation for and he still puts up with me. A majority of the positive characteristics in my life come from him because he was there at the foundation and is still guiding me. I am proud to say he is still my guide as are some of my closest friends Ziad, Haysam, Kodi and Saad. A special thanks to my Newport community brothers and sisters and dear close friends that I love so much not ranked in order including, Mo Bakkar, Marwan DJ Bliss and Danya, Badge, Zig, Wally, Taha El-Kurdi, Abdul Rahman Ramo Risilia, Youssef and Ahmad Dandash, Costa Lichoudaris, Abed Agha, Rania Hamadeh, Sam Eid, Anis and Hana Jallaf, Samantha Cameron, Hanks, Bu Zaid brothers, Luke Houli, Omar Souki, Bachar Houli, Mo Houli, Selim Houli, Sinan Ufuk, Gilbert Chami, Khaled Galal, Bec Hablos, Sara, Chris and Ellie, TD, Bassem Said, Roula Fares, Seba and Di, George Arc, Chris Anstee, Helen and Alan and too many to mention. Also, thanks to my other music business peeps, DJ's, venue managers, promoters, and friends you know who you are. To my elite mental coaching and biz friends there are many spiritual gangsters who helped on the way with their wisdom and love including Andrea Gullick, Niaz Hikmet, Hisham Dirbas, Tima ElHaj, Sandra, Shayoon and more. To my soccer and dear Carlton friends and peeps, Rashard, Zal, Shay, Suzie Belli, Rocco, Mars, Paulo, Sam Al Mouchi, Issan Joud, Amanda Groves, Lana, Jeana, Angie & Michael Edgely, Aaron, Bangkok Joe, and Vince. Go Blues!

To my extended yet small Hussein & Nesserdin family R.I.P mum and dad, my beautiful daughter Sarah, Dana and Nada. To my special Uncle Badir R.I.P who died a couple of years ago, he was my second father, my Aunty Jamila, Moemin and fam, Kaled and Fam, Ali and Haylz, Mimz and Sarwet and fam & to the El Hussein family Lina, Roula, Nini, Haifa, Aya, Moey, Issa, Moussa, I love you all.

BIOGRAPHY
Richard Rashid Hussein
ENTERTAINMENT

25 years+ experience between Australia & Dubai in the entertainment, business, and mind fitness fields. Richard Rashid has extensive experience with global companies in all thing's entertainment, he was the executive producer/A&R for The Voice, X factor & Coke Studio Middle East, and has worked with and consulted various leading multinational organisations, including Coca-Cola, Apple, Sony, Universal, Emirates Airlines, etc.

Richard has been working in the music industry since 1996 from BMG, Jive records to EMI Music Australia. He worked as the director at EMI Group MENA in 2006, which partnered up with and licensed some of the biggest local and international brands including Warner Music, Relax in, Virgin Records, Capitol Records, Free Music, Mazzika, Disney Music, M.O.S.

In addition, he's worked with major celebrities including Will Smith, Backstreet Boys, Coldplay, Jason Derulo, RedOne, Quincy Jones and major Arabic Artists such as Asala, Myriam Fares, Hamaki, etc.

Richard has achieved over 50 #1 best-selling regional products, collectively over 200 million views on YouTube and he was responsible for licensing music in Hollywood blockbusters (Sex in the City, Green Zone, Coco, Here and Now TV series etc.) and various TVC publishing music clearances. He also has an experience of 25+ years as International Professional DJ (DXB/MEL)

MIND FITNESS TRANsFORMER

Richard has worked with various high-performance individuals, artists, athletes, teams and organisations in coaching, leadership and team building. Some techniques and programs include effective communication, visualisation to break bad habits.

- Bachar Houli (Richmond Football Club) - 3 times premiership & All Australian AFL Star.
- Bachar Houli Foundation - as the mental coach for 15–18-year-old potential Australian Football League draftees.
- Brent Hayden - 4x Canadian Swimming Olympian, Olympic Medallist, World Champion.
- Greg Diesel Williams - 4x All Australian, AFL Dual Brownlow Medallist & AFL Premiership star, CFC Hall of Fame.

BUSINESS CONSULTANCY

In the corporate consultancy business, Richard's role focuses on strategic creation, planning and implementation in entertainment, coaching, training, speaking and operation structure with corporate leaders and managers. Various programs include negotiation skills, NLP coaching and leadership. Key clients include the Learning Initiative Dubai, Al Futtain, Bytedance, Tik Tok, Zaini Media etc.

ACADEMIC BACKGROUND

- B.A Music Business Management 2003 (R.M.I.T University)
- Master of Business Marketing 2007 (R.M.I.T University)
- International Golden Key Honorary Society member
- Certified NLP Practitioner & Hypnotist 2015 (R.S.C.I)

To contact Richard Rashid Hussein,
Please email @ RICHARDHUSSEIN1@GMAIL.COM

www.ingramcontent.com/pod-product-compliance
Lightning Source LLC
Chambersburg PA
CBHW031921240526
45464CB00021B/631